A YEAR OF MINI-MEDITATIONS
TO MANIFEST YOUR BEST LIFE

Dear
UNIVERSE
365

SARAH PROUT

HARVEST
An Imprint of WILLIAM MORROW

FOR MY MOTHER,

Louise

CONTENTS

INTRODUCTION

rayer and meditation are the art of communicating with the invisible realms, connecting you to the field of infinite potential that surrounds us all. As a manifestation teacher for over fifteen years, I've seen the transformative power of these practices firsthand. When paired with gratitude for whatever you are experiencing—whether it's joy, pain, grief, or transition—you can rise above even the toughest seasons of your life. This simple yet profound practice is at the heart of *Dear Universe 365*, a guide designed to help you connect to the Universe's power, align with your true self, and manifest your best life one day at a time.

This book was created during one of the most difficult and transformative chapters of my life. I found myself living under the same roof as my husband of ten years, facing the emotional turmoil of separation, yet still showing up each day for my children, my work, and myself. You'd think that spending the summer of 2024 in the Hamptons would be a luxurious dream, but for me, it became a crucible—a space where I was forced to confront my deepest fears, heartaches, and desires. On a quiet morning just before dawn, as I packed my bags to leave the home to live in a separate residence in another state, I was filled with a surprising sense of gratitude for all that had unfolded. This was the beginning of a profound healing journey, and it all started with the awareness that I needed to become who I knew I was meant to be.

For anyone who has ever had to make the hard decision to leave behind what is familiar—to end a relationship, walk away from a job, or let go of a version of yourself that no longer serves you—you know how daunting it can be. You live in a world of indecision, wondering if you're doing the right thing, and often grieving the life you thought you'd have. Writing this book was my way of navigating that uncertainty. Each "power word" became a lifeline, anchoring me in moments of doubt and guiding me toward the light, even on the darkest of days. This book is not just about my journey; it's about offering you the same support, no matter what transitions or challenges you may face throughout life.

THE LAW OF ATTRACTION: ENERGY AWARENESS AND INTUITIVE POWER

At the core of this transformative journey is the Law of Attraction—a universal principle that goes far beyond simple wishful thinking. It's an awareness of the energetic connection between all things, a recognition that we are not separate from the Universe but an integral part of its flowing consciousness. This law teaches us that like attracts like, not just in terms of positive thoughts attracting positive outcomes, but in the deeper sense of energetic alignment.

When you tune in to this universal frequency, you begin to notice the subtle whispers of your intuition—those gentle nudges and quiet knowings that guide you toward your highest good. The Law of Attraction isn't about forcing outcomes or maintaining artificial positivity; it's about becoming aware of the energy you're emanating and learning to align it with your deepest truths. Through this awareness, you develop a natural ability to attract experiences that resonate with your authentic self, your heart and your soul.

In times of transition or challenge, this principle becomes especially powerful. By maintaining awareness of your energetic state and choosing to align with higher frequencies—even while honoring your current emotions—you create a bridge between where you are and where you want to be. This isn't about denying your feelings but about understanding that even in darkness, you can hold space for the light.

THE MAGIC OF POWER WORDS

Each day in *Dear Universe 365* centers around a carefully chosen "power word"—a single term that serves as both an anchor and an invitation.

These aren't just ordinary words; they are energetic keys that unlock specific frequencies within your consciousness. A power word is a focal point for your daily meditation, a crystallized intention that helps you embody particular qualities or energies you wish to manifest.

When you encounter each day's power word, you're being invited to do more than just understand its meaning intellectually. You're being called to embody its essence, to let its vibration resonate through your entire being. Whether the word is trust, bravery, or joy, it becomes a mantra for your day, a lens through which to view your experiences, and a reminder of the energy you're choosing to align with.

These power words work in harmony with the Law of Attraction, creating a focused point of energetic attraction. By meditating on and embodying these words, you naturally begin to attract experiences that match their frequency. They become touchstones you can return to throughout your day, especially in moments when you need to realign with your intentions or find your center in the midst of chaos.

Unlike my previous book, *Dear Universe: 200 Mini-Meditations for Instant Manifestations,* which shared my personal story in depth, *Dear Universe 365* was written from a place of channeled wisdom that flowed through me during those pivotal moments. It's less about my narrative and more about the universal truths that helped me, and can now help you, find strength, clarity, and purpose during times of change. I wanted this book to meet you exactly where you are, whether you are grieving a loss, navigating a transition, on a healing journey, or wanting to take your life experience to a whole new and exciting level.

THE JOURNEY BEGINS

The Hamptons in New York provided the backdrop for my healing and was where I wrote this book—a place of serene beauty where nature's magic seemed to mirror my own unfolding. From the ancient trees that whispered stories of resilience to the sunsets that painted the sky with hope, the environment became my sanctuary. It wasn't just about the picturesque landscapes; it was about finding stillness in the chaos and reclaiming my sense of self. This journey was not just about finding answers but about learning to embrace the unknown, trusting that every ending is also a new beginning.

But let's be honest—this is not about bypassing your pain or pretending everything is okay when it isn't. Life is filled with bittersweet moments, and healing isn't a straight line. It's messy, it's raw, and sometimes, it feels impossible. There will be days when you feel overwhelmed, heartbroken, or unsure of your next step. This book isn't here to fix those feelings but to remind you that it's okay to feel them. It's okay to grieve, to be angry, to be uncertain. What matters is that you keep moving forward, one step, one breath, one moment at a time.

Dear Universe 365 is your companion through the storm. It's structured to support you, whether you're looking for daily guidance or seeking solace during moments of crisis. Each day offers a "power word" paired with a mini-meditation, encouraging you to set your intention and guide your thoughts toward healing and growth. These words are not just words; they are gentle reminders that even in your most fragile state, you are powerful beyond measure and you have the ability to manifest your best life.

YOU CAN USE THIS BOOK IN ONE OF TWO WAYS:

AS A DAY-BY-DAY SYSTEM FOR SUCCESS. Commit to a full year of personal growth and manifestation with a daily mini-meditation practice. This path empowers you to remember that feelings become things when you connect with the Universe. This structured approach provides a consistent framework for cultivating positive emotions and aligning with your true self. Tune in to a word each day and meditate on how you can embody the energy of the daily theme. You don't have to start on January 1st; begin whenever you're ready and make each day count as you feel inspired.

AS A DIP-IN, DIP-OUT ORACLE RESOURCE. Ask the Universe to guide you, and turn to any page to receive a message of wisdom. This flexible approach allows you to access guidance and inspiration whenever you need it, without the pressure of a daily commitment. Whether you're seeking comfort in a moment of grief, direction in a time of transition, or simply a reminder of your own strength, you can find the support you need right here.

Through my own journey of loss, change, and renewal, I've learned that the most profound transformations happen when we align with our true selves and live with intention. It's not about avoiding the hard stuff; it's about facing it with courage, grace, and a deep sense of gratitude for the lessons that come our way.

I hope that *Dear Universe 365* becomes a guiding light on your path—a source of comfort, inspiration, and strength as you navigate your own journey. Embrace the power of gratitude, allow yourself to feel every emotion, and trust that the Universe is always guiding you, even when the way forward seems unclear. You have the power to heal, to transform, and to create a life that feels true to who you are. Let this book be your reminder of that truth.

With Love & Gratitude,
SARAH PROUT
www.SarahProut.com
IG: @sarahprout

MONTH 1

gratitude and appreciation

On your journey of manifestation and personal growth, cultivating gratitude is essential for attracting abundance and joy. This month, we focus on developing a practice of gratitude and appreciation, opening your heart to the blessings that surround you.

Gratitude transforms your mindset, helping you recognize the positives in every situation and enhancing your overall well-being. By appreciating what you have, you align yourself with the energy of abundance and invite more good things into your life.

REMEMBER: Gratitude is a powerful tool in your manifestation toolkit. Embrace it daily and watch as your life fills with joy and positivity.

1

gratitude

IN THE MYSTICAL DANCE OF LIFE, gratitude is a transformative force, turning the ordinary into the extraordinary. It's not just an emotion, but a sacred alchemy that aligns us with the Universe's rhythm. Through gratitude, every sunrise becomes a canvas of hope, every breath a whisper of life's magic.

Gratitude is our soul's silent prayer, resonating with cosmic harmony. It unlocks the Universe's wonders, inviting abundance and aligning our hearts with the subtle beauties of existence. This level of gratitude is more than a fleeting feeling; it's a state of being, a perpetual wonder at the Universe's framework of existence. Gratitude unlocks the fullness of life, showing us a world waiting to be cherished.

DEAR UNIVERSE, today I open my heart to gratitude, acknowledging life's blessings in every moment. I am connected to the world's wonders, ready to receive and cherish the abundance that gratitude reveals. Thank you for this miraculous existence.

so be it,
so it is.

appreciation

APPRECIATION GOES BEYOND MERE GRATITUDE—it's not just about thanking someone for what we receive, but recognizing them for who they truly are. Consider this scenario: As a teenager, I often ignored the effort my mum put into laundering and neatly arranging clothes on my bed, only to toss them onto the floor. I took her for granted with my "floor-drobe" approach. It was only when I had my own teenage children that I truly appreciated my mother for the frustration she must have experienced as a result of my thoughtlessness.

Feeling appreciated means more than a thank-you; it involves a deep acknowledgment of someone's unique qualities and contributions. It's about valuing individuals not just for their actions but for their entire being.

Offering appreciation transcends mere thanks—it's about celebrating the quirks, skills, and essence of others. While gratitude says, "Thanks for what you did," appreciation says, "I see you, and you're incredible." It's a relationship builder and a culture creator that fosters respect and acknowledgment.

Who will you appreciate today?

DEAR UNIVERSE,
I embrace the power of appreciation, recognizing the uniqueness in others and myself. I am thankful for my connections and radiate positivity through appreciation.

so be it,
so it is.

DAY 3

blessed

YOU ARE BLESSED BEYOND MEASURE, even in moments when it might not feel that way. Each breath you take is a testament to life's endless possibilities and the many paths open before you. Consider the miracles surrounding you—friendships that nurture, challenges that strengthen, and unexpected moments of grace. You are a magnet for blessings, drawing toward you an abundance of goodness and light. Each day carries its own gifts, waiting for you to uncover them. Recognize these blessings, and let gratitude fill your heart, amplifying the goodness that flows in and out of your life.

DEAR UNIVERSE, may I recognize and cherish how blessed I am. May the multitude of blessings that enrich my life fill me with gratitude and love.

so be it,
so it is.

You can count your blessings by starting with the simplest joys: the warmth of sunlight on your skin, a good meal, a smile from a stranger. Each day offers gifts waiting to be noticed. Pause often, look around, and cherish the ordinary moments that weave the extraordinary tapestry of your life. Acknowledging these blessings not only cultivates gratitude but also transforms how you see your world, turning what you have into more than enough. You are so blessed.

thankful

YOU, IN YOUR ESSENCE, are a vessel of thankfulness. With each sunrise, remind yourself of the infinite reasons to be grateful. Life's smallest comforts—a warm cup of tea, a kind word, the softness of dawn—are reasons to feel profound thanks. The challenges, too, serve their purpose, molding you into your best self, revealing strength and resilience. As you embrace this mindset of thankfulness, you find that your life reflects more reasons to be grateful, creating a beautiful cycle of recognition and appreciation. Let thankfulness be your constant companion, coloring your days with positivity and peace.

Simply put, what you hold in your heart to be grateful for is a powerful and strong signal to the Universe to send you more things to appreciate. Thankfulness is the key to raising your frequency and aligning with your heart's desires.

DEAR UNIVERSE, instill in me a heart that is thankful for both the bounty and the lessons of life, enriching my spirit and guiding my path.

so be it, so it is.

joy

JOY IS NOT JUST AN EMOTION; it's a choice and a practice. It resides in the small, everyday moments as much as in life's grand triumphs. Choose to embrace joy in your morning smile, in the laughter shared with friends, when your dog runs around in circles in sheer excitement to see you, or in the accomplishment of your creative endeavors. By choosing joy, you invite an energy that uplifts not only your spirit but also those around you. Let this joy be infectious, a beacon that lights up your world and inspires others to find their own sparks of happiness. Embrace this radiant energy and let it transform every ordinary day into something extraordinary.

Activate the energy of joy by engaging in activities that make your heart sing. Whether it's dancing to your favorite song, listening to your favorite music, or walking in nature, choose actions that fill you with delight. Laugh loudly, embrace playfulness, and share these moments with others. Joy grows when shared, creating a ripple effect that enriches your life and those around you. Remember, joy is not just a feeling; it's an active choice and a radiant force that you can summon every day.

DEAR UNIVERSE, let joy permeate every aspect of my life, inspiring me to spread happiness and positivity wherever I go.

so be it, so it is.

reciprocity

THE LAW OF RECIPROCITY IS NOT just a guiding principle but a way of engaging with the world that can profoundly transform your life. It teaches you that the energy you send out into the Universe (without expectation) is the energy that returns, often magnified and adorned with the unexpected gifts of life.

In a small town on Long Island, New York, Laura owned a cozy café. One winter morning, a weary traveler named Jane came in, cold and out of money. Laura offered her a free hot chocolate and a place to stay. Jane was deeply grateful and promised to repay her.

Weeks later, Jane, a travel writer, returned to the café. She wrote an article about Laura's kindness, which was published in a popular magazine. Soon, travelers flocked to her café, boosting her business. Laura's simple act of kindness came full circle, showing how giving from the heart can bring unexpected rewards. This story illustrates the beauty of reciprocity.

DEAR UNIVERSE, I give freely and with love acknowledging the energy of reciprocity. I trust that your abundant flow will return this energy to me in miraculous and unexpected ways.

so be it, so it is.

7

serenity

SERENITY IS MORE THAN JUST FLEETING MOMENTS OF CALM—it is a profound state of peace that you cultivate within yourself, irrespective of the chaos around you. It is the gentle power that comes from understanding that you can navigate life's storms with ease, grace, and resilience. This inner tranquility does not signify the absence of conflict or difficulty; rather, it represents your ability to remain balanced and composed amid life's inevitable ups and downs.

It's like the old saying: "When life gives you lemons, make lemonade."

To embrace serenity, you must first accept the impermanence of all things. The challenges that unsettle you today will eventually pass, and new joys will take their place. By recognizing this ebb and flow, you learn to appreciate the present moment without clinging to it or fearing its departure.

DEAR UNIVERSE,
I seek serenity within me, embracing calm and clarity as I navigate life's flow, grounded in peace and guided by the gentle strength of my spirit.

so be it,
so it is.

Mindfulness is a key practice in cultivating serenity. It involves paying attention to your thoughts and emotions without judgment, allowing you to respond to life's complexities with wisdom rather than to react impulsively. Each mindful breath you take is a step toward deeper peace.

hope

ONE OF THE TOUGHEST EMOTIONAL SEASONS of my life was when I suffered five miscarriages in just ten months. With each subsequent loss, my faith and hope felt a little more diminished. I fell in love with each of the tiny heartbeats and decided to declare that as long as there is life, there is hope.

In the depths of my despair, I learned that hope is not just a fleeting feeling; it's a force, a profound determination to hold on even when the odds seem insurmountable. Each time I faced the heartache, I chose to embrace hope, not as a passive wish, but as an active stance against despair. It became my anchor, grounding me amid the turbulent waves of grief and loss. When I was pregnant with my daughter Lulu Dawn, hope was practiced in celebrating milestones and taking one day at a time until the moment my beautiful rainbow baby was safe in my arms in 2015.

Hope taught me resilience. It showed me that even when life strips you of what you hold dear, the human spirit's capacity to renew and find meaning remains unbroken. I began to see each day not as a reminder of what I had lost but as an opportunity to cherish what remains and to nurture possibilities, however uncertain they might seem.

DEAR UNIVERSE,
I embrace hope as my guiding light, believing that each new day holds infinite potential and the promise of a brighter, more joyful future.

so be it,
so it is.

awareness

CULTIVATING AWARENESS IS A PROFOUND JOURNEY that invites you to experience life more fully. It begins with you taking a step back to observe the intricacies of your thoughts, emotions, and surroundings without judgment or preconceived notions. This practice is about becoming an attentive witness to your own life, allowing you to recognize patterns, embrace growth, and navigate your path with intention.

Start by tuning in to your senses. Notice the texture of the air on your skin, the subtle flavors in your food, the colors and shapes that fill your vision, the scent of flowers in the springtime. These details ground you in the present moment—a fundamental aspect of cultivating awareness.

Remember, cultivating awareness is not about achieving a perfect state of mindfulness, but rather about deepening your understanding of yourself and your reactions to the world around you. As you become more aware, you might find that you respond to challenges with greater calm and make decisions more aligned with your values and goals. There is tremendous power in stopping to smell the roses (so to speak).

Embrace this journey of self-discovery with kindness and curiosity. Each moment of awareness adds a layer of depth to your life, transforming ordinary experiences into opportunities for real connection and profound insight.

DEAR UNIVERSE,
I invite heightened awareness into my life, seeking clarity and insight in every moment, and embracing each experience as an opportunity to learn and grow.

so be it,
so it is.

inspiration

FEELING INSPIRED IS LIKE CATCHING A SPARK that sets your soul alight with possibilities. It's a burst of energy that propels you toward creativity, innovation, and transformation. For you, inspiration might be as simple as feeling your coffee kick in in the morning and getting a boost of energy to work on a creative idea.

For me, inspiration tends to strike when I least expect it. In fact, many of my best ideas happen when I'm in the shower. There's something about running water that resets my soul and allows for the ideas to flow to me in a clearer way.

To harness this dynamic energy, pay attention to what stirs your spirit. Maybe it's nature, music, a good book, or conversations with loved ones.

Keep a journal or a note-taking app handy to capture your thoughts and ideas as they come. These snippets of inspiration can grow into projects, art, or changes in your life.

Let inspiration flow freely in your life. Welcome it, nurture it, and watch as it transforms your day-to-day existence, turning the ordinary into the extraordinary.

DEAR UNIVERSE,
I open my heart and mind to the infinite sources of inspiration around me, ready to transform creativity into action and dreams into reality.

*so be it,
so it is.*

awe

YOU STAND AT THE EDGE OF INFINITE POSSIBILITIES, each more profound than the last. Imagine the vast Universe, with its countless stars and galaxies, and remember that you are part of this magnificent creation. We are all part of the same fabric of Oneness. You are not just a spectator but a participant in the grand tapestry of existence. Feel the awe wash over you as you contemplate the mysteries of the cosmos, the beauty of a sunrise, or the complexity of your own soul. Let this awe inspire you to live fully, embracing each moment with the reverence it deserves.

If you feel inspired, make a list of all the ways you have felt a sense of awe in your life. For me it's things like looking into my beloved's eyes, holding a newborn baby in my arms, when trees start to blossom after a long cold winter, the feeling of applying paint to a fresh canvas . . . the list goes on! Revisit your list often to remember what activates this powerful energy within you.

DEAR UNIVERSE, guide me to always stand in awe of the everyday miracles, and let this wonder fuel my journey through life with manifestation, miracles, and magic.

so be it,
so it is.

compassion

COMPASSION IS YOUR SUPERPOWER. It serves as a profound connection to others, allowing you to deeply empathize with their joys and sorrows, experiencing them as if they were your own. In a world where everyone carries unseen burdens, your acts of kindness can shine as beacons of hope in the darkness. Let your heart remain open, and your actions considerate. Compassion not only has the potential to change the world—it transforms you from within.

Moreover, living compassionately involves recognizing our shared humanity. It calls on you to forgive, to be patient, and to offer the same kindness to yourself as you would to others. Through this practice, you not only help heal others but also nurture your own soul, cultivating a peaceful inner world. What is something compassionate that you could do for someone else today?

DEAR UNIVERSE, fill my heart with boundless compassion, that I may be a source of comfort and light to all I encounter. May I embody love and light, inspiring the same in others.

so be it,
so it is.

13

healing

HEALING IS A PROFOUND JOURNEY, not merely a destination. It's about finding serenity within our scars, embracing them, not attempting to erase them. Early in 2023, I faced a personal challenge when I was diagnosed with basal cell carcinoma on my right cheek. The Mohs surgery necessary to remove it left a visible scar, a constant reminder on my face that healing is an ongoing process. This scar initially shook my self-esteem—after all, my appearance is part of my professional presence as an author. Yet, this experience became a powerful invitation from the Universe to delve deeper and heal not just physically but emotionally, addressing the insecurities tied to my self-image.

DEAR UNIVERSE, grant me the strength to embrace healing, to learn from my pain, and to grow stronger in the broken places.

so be it, so it is.

Healing teaches us to embrace our imperfections and recognize that each wound, whether seen or unseen, brings its own wisdom and strength. It's about healing at your pace, acknowledging that every step forward is part of a transformative journey toward wholeness. Remember, you are never alone in your healing when you connect with the Universe.

optimism

OPTIMISM IS THE FAITH THAT LEADS TO ACHIEVEMENT. It allows you to see beyond the horizon, to imagine a brighter day ahead even in the darkest of times. Cultivate a mindset that embraces possibilities, and let hope illuminate your path. When you believe that the best is yet to come, you open yourself up to receive it.

You stand on the brink of endless possibilities. Every challenge you've faced has been a stepping stone, preparing you for greater achievements. Remember, growth often comes disguised as obstacles, and you've learned from each one. The best is yet to come because you are continually evolving, gaining wisdom, and embracing opportunities that your past self could only dream about. With each day, you're becoming stronger and more capable. Your future is not just a continuation of your past; it's an exciting, uncharted journey filled with potential triumphs. Believe in your journey, for the most rewarding chapters of your life await.

DEAR UNIVERSE, infuse my spirit with optimism, that I may always see the silver lining and embrace the endless possibilities of tomorrow. The best is yet to come.

so be it,
so it is.

15

playfulness

PLAYFULNESS ISN'T JUST FOR CHILDREN. It's a way of engaging with the world that sparks creativity and joy. Allow yourself to laugh, to dance, to play. These moments of lightheartedness rejuvenate your soul and remind you that life, despite its complexities, is meant to be enjoyed. Rediscover the playful spirit within you and let it color your days.

At the time I am writing this, I live a short walk away from the private community beach here in Southampton, New York. Near the beautiful shoreline is a playground with a set of swings overlooking the gorgeous and historic Peconic Bay, which was first settled in 1640. One morning, with no one around, I decided that I needed to sit on the swings, kick my legs, and get as high as I used to when I was a small girl who loved the thrill of a playground. The thing I noticed the most was that I felt the same way I did at forty-four as I did when I was seven years old. I would see my feet try to touch the clouds and feel a sense of freedom and playfulness in the present moment.

DEAR UNIVERSE, awaken the spirit of playfulness within me, that I may enjoy the dance of life with a light heart and joyful steps.

so be it,
so it is.

As much as you can, seek out these kinds of experiences to do away with stale old rules that stop you from having fun as an adult. Your spirit will be allowed the space to shine.

wonder

WONDER IS THE BEGINNING OF WISDOM. Let yourself be curious, ask questions, and explore the world with the eyes of a child. The world is a magical place, teeming with wonders waiting to be discovered by those who dare to look. Let this sense of wonder lead you to discoveries both external and internal.

However, to activate the best energy of wonder, you need to be good or at least comfortable at asking questions—questions for understanding and for self-discovery. This helps to anchor and activate new levels of awareness.

DEAR UNIVERSE, keep my sense of wonder alive, that I may continually be enchanted and inspired by the world around me.

so be it, so it is.

17

bliss

BLISS IS YOUR SOUL'S WAY OF telling you that you're exactly where you need to be. Embrace moments of bliss, those deep, serene experiences of complete happiness and contentment. These moments are your life's true treasures. Savor them, store them in your heart, and recall them in times of need.

> **DEAR UNIVERSE,** let my life be filled with moments of bliss, reminding me of the profound beauty and peace that exists within and around me.
>
> *so be it, so it is.*

Bliss to me is when the water in the local bay looks like glass at sunset. The air is warm and there is a gentle breeze. I have bare feet standing on the sand watching my two youngest daughters run around and play with smiles on their faces.

delight

DELIGHT IN THE SMALL JOYS—like the first bite of a decadent dessert, the sound of birds chirping at dawn, or the feel of warm sunshine on your skin. Imagine the refreshing taste of a cold lemonade on a hot summer day or the cozy comfort of a favorite blanket on a chilly evening. These bits of happiness weave a tapestry of delight that can envelop your everyday life. Let yourself be delighted, and you will find joy in the most unexpected places.

Embrace the tiny wonders that each day holds. As you pay attention to these fleeting moments, your senses sharpen, deepening your appreciation for life's simple pleasures. This newfound awareness invites a lighter, more joyful presence into your days, uplifting your spirit and enriching your interactions with others. Let the mundane become magical and watch as your world transforms with the vibrant colors of joy and gratitude.

On a personal note, some of my favorite people that I enjoy spending time with enjoy the tiny moments in life. Whether it's making a delicious salad or sharing a laugh, the energy of delight is tiny but mighty.

DEAR UNIVERSE, may I find delight in every day, discovering joy and beauty in the smallest of moments and the simplest of pleasures.

so be it, so it is.

19

fulfillment

YOU HOLD THE KEY TO YOUR OWN FULFILLMENT. It lies in recognizing the beauty of your individual journey and in valuing the moments, big and small, that make up your life. Embrace your passions, engage with your community, and let every experience enrich you. Fulfillment doesn't come from external achievements alone but from a deep, personal alignment with your actions and beliefs. Savor the process as much as the outcomes. Each step you take is a thread in the vibrant tapestry of your life, woven with joy, learning, and satisfaction.

DEAR UNIVERSE, help me to weave my tapestry of life with threads of joy, fulfillment, and purpose.

so be it, so it is.

Cultivate a spirit of gratitude, and watch how it transforms everyday experiences into profound insights. One day you will feel grounded and embodied with how fulfilled you feel. Even if you never thought it would happen, you'll find that it was worth the wait.

peace

FIND YOUR PEACE IN THE QUIET moments between the hustle of daily duties. It resides in the deep breaths you take when you pause, in the soft whispers of nature, and in the gentle closure of your eyes at night. Peace is an internal haven that you can visit anytime you choose. It shields you from life's chaos and cocoons you in calmness. Cultivate this sanctuary within by forgiving past hurts and releasing future worries. Let peace be your steadfast companion, guiding you through life's storms with serenity and strength.

One of the ways I love to find peace and stillness is by being in nature. In particular by sitting by the sea and watching the light on the water's surface. It brings me a profound sense of peace.

DEAR UNIVERSE, grant me the calmness and clarity that come with true peace.

so be it, so it is.

21

trust

TRUST YOURSELF. TRUST THE JOURNEY. Trust that each experience has a purpose, even if it's not clear in the moment. Build trust by listening to your intuition, honoring your promises, and staying true to your values. Trust fosters deeper connections and opens the door to meaningful opportunities. Let go of the need for certainty, and embrace the beauty of becoming. With trust, you can navigate the unknown with confidence and grace, knowing that you are exactly where you need to be.

If you're human, then at some point in your life your levels of trust will either be broken or tested. Don't let this define you because trust always begins with self-trust.

DEAR UNIVERSE, deepen my trust in the path ahead and in the lessons I learn along the way.

so be it,
so it is.

Trust is not just a gift we give to others; it is also a gift we give to ourselves. When we trust, we release the weight of suspicion and doubt, freeing our minds and hearts to focus on what truly matters. We cultivate peace within and inspire those around us to do the same.

confidence

CONFIDENCE IS YOUR INNATE RIGHT. CLAIM IT. Stand tall with the knowledge of your worth and let your actions reflect your inner certainty. Confidence isn't about knowing you'll never fail, but about believing in your ability to rise after falling. It's the voice that speaks boldly and the heart that doesn't waver under scrutiny. Nurture your confidence by setting boundaries, celebrating your achievements, and embracing challenges as opportunities to grow. With confidence, you can chart the course of your life with daring and purpose. Stand tall, stand in your power, and trust that you always have access to the energy of confidence when you need it most.

I was always quite a shy child, and when I trained myself in the art of public speaking on stages around the world, it helped to build my confidence. This will always happen when you are willing to venture outside of your comfort zone.

DEAR UNIVERSE,
infuse my actions with confidence and my decisions with courage.

so be it,
so it is.

23

kindness

KINDNESS IS THE PUREST FORM OF connection between souls. It transcends language and culture, touching hearts and transforming lives. Be kind to yourself—acknowledge your struggles, celebrate your strengths, and forgive your missteps. We're human and sometimes we make mistakes! It's okay. Always remember to be kind to yourself. Extend this kindness outward, for every act of compassion echoes into infinity. In a world that often prioritizes self-interest, choose to be the light of kindness. It's a choice that not only changes others but also redefines your own life's experience, filling it with warmth and love.

Inspired action: Commit a random act of kindness today and make someone smile.

DEAR UNIVERSE,
let my life be
a reflection of
kindness and
compassion to all.

so be it,
so it is.

belongingness

YOU ARE AN INTEGRAL PART OF a greater whole, connected to a web of beings and energies that can support and uplift you. Belongingness isn't just about being included; it's about knowing that you inherently fit into the vast puzzle of the Universe. When you think of it this way, it can feel so magical. Look around and see the connections in your daily interactions, feel the bonds with those who share your journey, and know that you are never truly alone. This sense of belonging fuels a deep and abiding peace within your soul.

DEAR UNIVERSE, help me find and nurture my place among the incredible hearts that surround me. May I manifest the essence of belongingess and feel at home within myself.

so be it, so it is.

One of the ways to feel like you belong is to also make other people feel welcomed by your energy. It's always about creating a mutual support system and being willing to contribute to helping others find their place in the world too.

25

harmony

HARMONY IS THE SILENT MUSIC BETWEEN your life's notes. It's found when your inner world aligns with the outer, and actions and beliefs synchronize peacefully. Strive to create balance in your thoughts, relationships, and environment. As you do, you'll find that peace flows more freely, resonating through every aspect of your being.

Have you ever heard a song where two voices are beautifully harmonized? It creates deep spiritual resonance. About a year ago I decided to start singing. I've always hidden my singing voice because I didn't feel very confident. One day I decided to sing along to a song that a dear musician friend sent to me—and I recorded it and sent it to him to listen to! I felt super-self-conscious, but our voices perfectly harmonized and it was as if a new portal opened up in my soul that I had once kept very private and hidden. Harmony sometimes happens when we least expect it.

Harmonic resonance is really the key to manifestations. It's the complementary alignment of energy that produces a creative union.

DEAR UNIVERSE,
infuse my life with harmony, balancing my spirit, mind, and body to resonate with the universe's rhythm.

so be it,
so it is.

jubilation

JUBILATION IS A BURST OF JOY that fills your chest and spreads uncontrollably. It's that feeling when something wonderful happens or when you're surrounded by love and laughter. Cultivate these moments by appreciating the miracles in everyday life. Let jubilation not be a rare guest, but a familiar friend who visits often.

Celebrate your achievements, both big and small, and allow yourself to fully feel the joy they bring. Share your happiness with others, spreading jubilation wherever you go. When you choose to see the world through the lens of gratitude and positivity, you invite more moments of joy into your life. Let your heart be open to the beauty that surrounds you, and let jubilation be the soundtrack of your journey.

DEAR UNIVERSE, may my days be filled with jubilation, celebrating each moment's blessing with heartfelt joy.

so be it,
so it is.

27

amazement

EVERY DAY, LIFE OFFERS A CANVAS RICH IN WONDERS. Let yourself be amazed by the world's beauty and mysteries. From the intricacies of a leaf to the expanse of the night sky, amazement is the feeling of being fully alive and in awe of the Universe's magnificence.

I remember one night back in 2022, I was sitting in the jacuzzi in Sag Harbor, New York. It was an extraordinarily clear night and the stars looked like luminous whispers of the Universe, scattered across the velvet canvas of the night sky. Then all of a sudden a meteor shot over the horizon. It had a super-long tail and lit the sky as it left me in a state of awe and utter amazement. So many incredible moments of amazement unfold when you allow yourself to spend time in nature.

DEAR UNIVERSE, awaken a sense of amazement within me daily, as I witness the wonders of the world you've created.

so be it, so it is.

admiration

ADMIRATION IS THE RECOGNITION OF THE beauty and brilliance in others and the world around you. It's seeing the light in another's soul or the art in nature's design and feeling inspired. Let this admiration spur you toward personal growth and deeper connections.

My dad is an incredible watercolor artist. I grew up in galleries and studios around the world, and I would often witness the energy of deep admiration from the collectors of my father's paintings. The admiration was in how he could capture the light and essence of the places he was bringing to life through paint. Admiration is one of the kindest gifts you can share with an artist because the recognition can encourage them to keep creating.

DEAR UNIVERSE, let me always find admiration for the strength and beauty in others and myself, inspiring continuous growth and connection.

so be it, so it is.

29

graciousness

GRACIOUSNESS IS THE ART OF BEING KIND, humble, and patient, even when the world tempts you to react otherwise. It's about handling every interaction with dignity and extending kindness without expecting anything in return. Cultivate this trait, and watch how it transforms your life and touches those around you.

DEAR UNIVERSE, guide me with graciousness that I may handle every situation with kindness and humility.

so be it, so it is.

But let's face it, if you're just not feeling it, sometimes it can be hard to be gracious. My advice? Allow yourself to get out of your own way and watch the magic happen.

lightheartedness

LIGHTHEARTEDNESS IS LIKE THE BREEZE THAT lifts the leaves on a summer day—it's light and refreshing and effortlessly uplifts. Seek out moments that make your heart feel light, be it through humor, play, or simple pleasures. Let this lighthearted energy permeate your life, bringing ease and joy.

DEAR UNIVERSE, fill my days with lightheartedness, easing my journey with laughter and joyous moments.

I love to put on loud music and dance and sing with my two youngest daughters. This lifts all of our spirits and creates the instant energy of lightheartedness. Shake your booty!

so be it, so it is.

31

contentedness

CONTENTEDNESS IS THE DEEP, satisfying breath you take when life feels just right. It's appreciating what you have, where you are, and who you're with. This peace doesn't come from having everything but from appreciating everything you have. Nurture this sense of contentment, and let it ground you.

DEAR UNIVERSE, grant me the serenity of contentedness, to truly appreciate my life's current blessings and joys.

so be it, so it is.

Contentedness can be a deep sense of well-being and fulfillment, free from persistent longing for something more or different. For me it's always about sharing a present moment of gratitude with my family, friends, and loved ones.

MONTH 2
connection and relationships

Building meaningful connections and nurturing relationships are vital aspects of your personal growth journey. This month, we focus on deepening your bonds with others and fostering a sense of belonging and connection in the most magical of ways.

Strong relationships provide support, love, and encouragement, helping you stay aligned with your goals and dreams. By connecting with others on a deeper level, you create a network of positive energy that amplifies your manifestation efforts.

REMEMBER: Relationships are a reflection of the love and energy you give and receive. Cultivate connections that uplift and inspire you, and your journey will be enriched with mutual growth and fulfillment. And most importantly, always prioritize sharing laughter with others and watch the magic manifest.

friendship

WHO IS THE EARLIEST FRIEND YOU have memories of connecting with? For me, it's my friend Hadley. He was a little younger than I was when I was about three or four living in New Zealand. I have this random memory of sitting under a giant palm tree in our front yard and eating honey sandwiches. Shared joy is the measure of a true friendship.

You are a beacon of light in the lives of those around you. Friendship is the golden thread that binds us to the tapestry of life, enriching our journey with joy, support, and love. Cherish your friends, for they are the mirrors reflecting your true self, celebrating your victories and offering solace in times of sorrow. Remember, true friends are not just there for the sunny days but are the anchors that hold you steady during the storm. Nurture these bonds with kindness, honesty, and unwavering support. In friendship, you find a sanctuary, a place where your soul feels seen, heard, and understood. Embrace your friends with an open heart, and let the love you share be a testament to the beauty of human connection.

The best intention to hold is to always be a good friend, a person who is true to their word and offers support in someone's times of need. Simply put, if you want to manifest good friendships, you have to be willing to be a good friend.

DEAR UNIVERSE, thank you for the gift of true friendship, filled with love, support, and mutual understanding.

so be it, so it is.

community

YOU ARE AN INTEGRAL PART OF a greater whole, part of a global community that thrives on unity and mutual support. In community, we find strength, purpose, and a sense of belonging. Embrace your role within your community, knowing that your unique contributions make a significant impact. Foster connections with those around you, offering your skills, your time, and your compassion. Together, you create a network of support that can overcome any challenge and celebrate every triumph. Recognize the power of collective effort and the beauty of shared dreams. Your community is a living entity, growing and evolving with each act of kindness and cooperation. Stand tall within this circle of life, knowing you are never alone.

The sense of belonging that comes from being part of a community has profound effects on mental and emotional health. In times of hardship, communities provide a safety net of empathy, understanding, and practical support. This social connection is a vital component of human happiness and fulfillment. Find your people and cherish them as your soul family.

DEAR UNIVERSE,
I am grateful for the strength and unity of my community, and I vow to contribute my best.

so be it,
so it is.

3

empathy

YOU POSSESS THE INCREDIBLE GIFT OF EMPATHY, a bridge that connects hearts and minds. Empathy allows you to walk in another's shoes, to feel their joy, their pain, and their dreams. Embrace this gift, letting it guide you in your interactions with others. Show kindness and understanding, for everyone you meet is fighting a battle you may know nothing about. Through empathy, you create a ripple effect of compassion and love that touches lives in profound ways. Listen with your heart, offer your support, and be a source of comfort and strength. In practicing empathy, you not only uplift others but also elevate your own spirit, creating a world that is more connected, caring, and humane.

DEAR UNIVERSE, may my heart always be open to understanding and compassion, spreading love through empathy.

so be it, so it is.

Perhaps you see yourself as an empath? This heightened sensitivity allows you to be incredibly compassionate and intuitive, but it can also make you vulnerable to emotional overload and stress. It's important to understand how to manage your energy so that you can feel the feelings of others and still protect yourself at the same time.

bonding

YOU ARE CAPABLE OF FORMING DEEP and meaningful bonds that enrich your life and the lives of others. Bonding is the essence of human connection, the thread that weaves individuals into families, friends, and communities. It is through these bonds that we share our experiences, our dreams, and our vulnerabilities. Embrace the opportunity to connect with others on a profound level, sharing your authentic self and creating spaces for others to do the same. Whether it's through shared laughter, mutual support, or heartfelt conversations, these bonds provide a foundation of love and trust. Cherish the moments of closeness and let them remind you of the beauty of human connection.

DEAR UNIVERSE, thank you for the deep levels of bonding that fill my life with love and meaning.

so be it, so it is.

The bond I had with my grandmother is something I will cherish for eternity. Our bond was built upon mutual understanding and unconditional love.

5

affection

YOU HAVE AN INCREDIBLE CAPACITY TO give and receive affection, a force that nurtures the soul and warms the heart. Affection is the gentle touch, the kind word, and the loving gesture that speaks volumes. It is a powerful expression of love and care that can heal wounds and strengthen relationships.

Don't hesitate to show affection to those you love, for it is in these moments that true connections are made. Let your affection flow freely, creating a tapestry of love that wraps around you and those you cherish. Remember, a simple act of affection can make a world of difference in someone's day and in their life. Get intentional with hugging more people if you feel comfortable to do so. Hugs are a great way to show people you care and to connect with them on a deeper level.

DEAR UNIVERSE, may I always give and receive affection freely, spreading warmth and love wherever I go.

so be it, so it is.

unity

UNITY IS THE STRENGTH THAT ARISES when hearts and minds come together in harmony. It is the bond that transcends differences, creating a collective force that is greater than the sum of its parts. In unity, we find a shared purpose and a common vision, allowing us to achieve remarkable things. Embrace the spirit of unity by recognizing the interconnectedness of all beings and the beauty in diversity.

Sadly, we live in a time where there are certain powers that profit from us being disconnected from ourselves and one another. Always choose unity over separation and remember that everyone is on their own unique learning journey throughout life.

DEAR UNIVERSE,
I embrace unity, joining with others in harmony and strength to create a better world.

so be it, so it is.

When we stand united, in a unified paradigm, we are unstoppable, able to overcome any challenge and build a brighter future together.

companionship

COMPANIONSHIP IS THE GENTLE EMBRACE OF a loyal friend, the comfort of knowing you are never truly alone. It is the laughter shared until your face hurts, the tears wiped away, and the silent understanding that needs no words. It's the warmth of a hand held during a difficult moment, the inside joke that brings a smile with just a glance, and the peaceful silence of reading books side by side on a lazy Sunday afternoon.

Companionship is found in the late-night conversations that drift from the profound to the absurd, in the impromptu dance parties in your kitchen, and in the quiet act of making each other's favorite meal. It's the gentle nudge that encourages you to pursue your dreams, the unwavering support when you stumble, and the genuine celebration of your successes, no matter how small.

DEAR UNIVERSE,
I cherish and nurture the gift of companionship, finding joy and comfort in the presence of true friends and kindred spirits.

so be it,
so it is.

True companionship brings joy and warmth to your journey, making even the hardest paths more bearable. Cherish the bonds you have, and be a good (and hopefully entertaining) companion to others. In companionship, you find solace, support, and the profound beauty of human connection.

respect

RESPECT IS THE CORNERSTONE OF EVERY meaningful relationship, built on understanding, empathy, and recognition of each other's intrinsic worth. It is the silent nod of acknowledgment, the openhearted listening, and the mindful appreciation of differences. When you give respect, you cultivate an environment where trust and love can flourish.

Value yourself and others, treating everyone with kindness and dignity. In doing so, you create a world where respect becomes the norm, fostering deeper connections and greater harmony. Respect transcends cultural boundaries, serving as a universal language that bridges divides and promotes mutual understanding. It is both a personal choice and a collective responsibility, shaping the very fabric of our society and paving the way for a more compassionate world.

DEAR UNIVERSE,
may I practice respect in all my interactions, honoring the worth and dignity of myself and others.

so be it,
so it is.

9

cooperation

COOPERATION IS THE SYNERGY THAT ARISES when individuals unite their strengths and talents, creating something greater than any one person could achieve alone. Embrace cooperation by fostering a spirit of collaboration and mutual support. Celebrate the successes and learn from the challenges, knowing that together, you can overcome any obstacle and achieve remarkable things.

Think about what it feels like when someone doesn't want to cooperate—it can be extremely frustrating, so it's always a good idea to help out if you can. By being a team player and being willing to support others, you raise your vibration and accelerate your manifestations.

DEAR UNIVERSE, may I foster cooperation, working harmoniously with others to achieve our common goals.

so be it, so it is.

warmheartedness

WARMHEARTEDNESS IS THE RADIANT GLOW OF kindness and compassion that emanates from a loving soul. It is the gentle touch, the comforting word, and the sincere smile that lights up the lives of others. Being warmhearted means embracing empathy and generosity, spreading love and positivity wherever you go. Let your heart be a source of warmth and light, touching others with your genuine care and affection. In warmheartedness, you find the true essence of humanity and the joy of making a positive difference.

Have you ever met someone who was just so welcoming and friendly? Where you were made to feel at home in their presence? Cherish these people. They are rare unicorns.

DEAR UNIVERSE,
I embrace warmheartedness, spreading kindness and compassion to brighten the lives of those around me.

so be it,
so it is.

loyalty

ONE OF MY STRONGEST VALUES IS LOYALTY—in friendships, relationships, and above all to myself. I encourage you to practice being loyal to yourself too. Being loyal to yourself means consistently honoring your own needs, values, and boundaries over time. It involves prioritizing self-care, staying true to your core beliefs, setting healthy limits in relationships, and following through on personal commitments—all while treating yourself with compassion and advocating for your own growth and well-being. It's definitely a practice that requires awareness.

It is the unwavering support you give to those you cherish, the promise to stand by their side no matter what.

DEAR UNIVERSE,
I embody loyalty, standing steadfast and true in my commitments and relationships.

*so be it,
so it is.*

In a world that often changes, your loyalty is a rare and precious gift. Embrace loyalty by being dependable and true, showing up for the people who matter to you. Let your loyalty be a beacon of trust and love, strengthening your relationships and building unbreakable bonds. Only bonds that cannot be broken are built by the magic of loyalty.

understanding

WHEN WAS THE LAST TIME YOU told someone that you understand them? Understanding is a beautiful gift to give someone. It's a lovely acknowledgment that you know what they might be going through.

Understanding is the bridge that connects hearts and minds, fostering deep and meaningful relationships. It is the patience to listen, the empathy to feel, and the wisdom to see things from another's perspective. By cultivating understanding, you open the door to genuine connection and harmony. Take the time to truly listen and seek to comprehend others, even when it's difficult. Your understanding will create a space where love and trust can flourish.

DEAR UNIVERSE,
I cultivate understanding, listening with empathy and seeking to connect deeply with others.

so be it,
so it is.

13

altruism

ALTRUISM IS THE SELFLESS ACT OF GIVING without expecting anything in return. It is the purest form of love and kindness, a testament to the beauty of the human spirit. Embrace altruism by offering your time, resources, and compassion to those in need. Let your actions be guided by the desire to make the world a better place. Each act of altruism, no matter how small, creates ripples of positive change that extend far beyond your immediate reach.

DEAR UNIVERSE,
I practice altruism, giving selflessly and spreading kindness wherever I go.

so be it, so it is.

When I lived in Las Vegas, there was a local women's shelter that would call out for basic items like shampoo, soap, toothbrushes, and underwear. I made sure that I could help out whenever I was able to. By giving money, donations, or time, you are helping to raise the frequency of the planet with the energy of kindness.

support

MAY YOU FEEL SUPPORTED IN YOUR LIFE by the Universe. May you feel supported to build your dreams and overcome your challenges.

Support is the encouragement, the helping hand, and the belief in someone's potential. Be a pillar of support for those around you, offering your strength and understanding when they need it most. Your support can make all the difference in someone's life, giving them the courage to keep going.

Together, we rise higher and achieve more than we ever could alone.

DEAR UNIVERSE,
I offer unwavering support to those around me, helping them reach their fullest potential.

*so be it,
so it is.*

15

sympathy

SUFFERING IS ONE OF THE PITFALLS of being human. We all go through different seasons of struggle throughout life, which is why it's so important to acknowledge another's pain and the willingness to be present in their suffering. It is the soft touch, the kind word, and the compassionate heart that brings comfort to those in distress. Embrace sympathy by being there for others in their times of need, showing them that they are not alone. Your sympathetic presence can be a healing medicine, providing solace and understanding in moments of hardship.

DEAR UNIVERSE,
I extend my sympathy, offering comfort and compassion to those in need.

*so be it,
so it is.*

Your mission today is to be there for someone else who might need a sympathetic ear.

generosity

GENEROSITY IS A POWERFUL FORCE THAT not only transforms the lives of others but also enriches your own. When you give selflessly, you create a chain reaction of kindness and abundance. Acts of generosity, whether big or small, can bring immense joy and fulfillment. Share your time, resources, and compassion freely, knowing that what you give returns to you multiplied. Embrace a generous heart, and watch as your world blossoms with deeper connections and greater blessings.

It really doesn't take much to display a generous spirit, but it's always so lovely. My dear friend Catherine loves to bake and brings over delicious goodies from time to time. It's these acts of kindness that are beautiful expressions of generosity. Ask yourself: Are there some ways that you can be more generous to others in your life?

DEAR UNIVERSE,
I open my heart to generosity, sharing my abundance freely and creating ripples of kindness in the world.

so be it,
so it is.

17

togetherness

WHEN I FIRST MOVED TO AMERICA, I was blown away by the magic of the holidays that get celebrated here. Thanksgiving in particular seemed like a wonderful opportunity to create memories with friends and family. Even though I will likely never eat turkey (I prefer Tofurkey), when you share a meal with loved ones, it activates the essence of human connection and community.

DEAR UNIVERSE,
I cherish the spirit of togetherness, embracing unity and connection with those around me. We are stronger together.

so be it,
so it is.

When you come together with others, you create a sense of belonging and support that nurtures the soul. Celebrate the bonds that unite you, whether with family, friends, or your community. Embrace collaboration and shared experiences, knowing that together, you are stronger and more resilient. Cherish the moments of togetherness, and let them remind you of the power of unity and love.

charisma

HAVE YOU EVER MET ANYONE WHO just seems to ooze charisma?

Charisma is the radiant energy that attracts and inspires others. It is the confidence and magnetism that comes from being authentic and true to yourself. When you embrace your unique qualities and shine your light, you naturally draw people to you.

Cultivate your charisma by believing in yourself, expressing your passions, and sharing your enthusiasm with the world. Let your inner light shine brightly, illuminating the path for yourself and others.

DEAR UNIVERSE,
I embrace my charisma, radiating confidence and authenticity, inspiring and attracting positivity.

so be it,
so it is.

19

reliability

AT TIMES I HAVE A LOT of anxiety about being late for meetings or appointments. I think it's because if I say I'm going to do something, then I do it. Being reliable is a way to connect with someone and show them that you respect their time. In fact, reliability is a cornerstone of trust and respect. When you are reliable, you become a pillar of strength and dependability for others. Your actions and words align, creating a foundation of trust in your relationships and endeavors.

Be consistent in your commitments, follow through on your promises, and show up with integrity. As you embody reliability, you build lasting connections and create a legacy of trustworthiness.

DEAR UNIVERSE,
I embody reliability, consistently showing up with integrity and trustworthiness in all my actions.

*so be it,
so it is.*

nurturing

TAKE A MOMENT TO PAUSE WITH gratitude for the people in your life who have helped to nurture you. Call them if you can, or say a silent prayer/ meditation to send the essence of gratitude in their direction.

Nurturing is the art of caring for yourself and others with love and compassion. It involves creating a supportive environment where growth and healing can flourish. Whether through kind words, thoughtful actions, or simply being present, your nurturing spirit can make a profound difference. Cultivate this quality by being gentle with yourself and extending that same care to those around you. Embrace the role of a nurturer, and watch as your world blossoms with love and vitality.

DEAR UNIVERSE, may I be nurturing to myself and others with love and compassion, fostering growth and healing in all areas of my life.

so be it, so it is.

21

mutuality

BY GIVING FREELY AND WITH LOVE, you open the flow of abundance to receive in return—this is the law of reciprocity in action.

Mutual respect and understanding form the foundation of meaningful and beautiful relationships. When you approach interactions with a spirit of mutuality, you create a balanced exchange where both parties feel valued, seen, and heard. This reciprocity fosters deeper connections and a sense of belonging. Embrace the concept of mutual support, where giving and receiving are in harmony. By recognizing and honoring the worth of others, you cultivate an environment of trust and cooperation, enriching both your life and theirs.

DEAR UNIVERSE,
I embrace mutuality and understanding in all my relationships, fostering deep and meaningful connections.

*so be it,
so it is.*

harmonious

WHEN YOU SEE THINGS FROM THE lens of harmony, then peace usually manifests fairly quickly.

Harmony is the art of living in balance with yourself and the world around you. When you cultivate a harmonious life, you align your thoughts, actions, and emotions with your true self. This alignment brings peace and contentment, allowing you to navigate challenges with grace. Strive for harmony in your relationships, your environment, and within yourself. By fostering balance and understanding, you create a life of tranquility and fulfillment.

DEAR UNIVERSE,
I create harmonious energy in my life, aligning my thoughts, actions, and emotions with my true self.

so be it,
so it is.

23

collaboration

WHEN YOU WORK WELL WITH OTHERS, it creates a magical energy.

Collaboration is the key to unlocking collective potential. When you join forces with others, you combine strengths, ideas, and resources to achieve greater results than you could ever imagine manifesting alone. Embrace the spirit of teamwork and open-mindedness, valuing the contributions of each person involved.

By working collaboratively, you foster innovation, support, and shared success. Celebrate the power of coming together and the remarkable outcomes that collaboration brings. Even if you are adamant that you are a lone wolf, try considering venturing out of your comfort zone to activate the energy of shared success. It's magical.

DEAR UNIVERSE,
I embrace collaboration, valuing the strengths and ideas of others to achieve shared success.

so be it,
so it is.

connectivity

IF YOU GREW UP BEFORE THE 2000S, then you likely remember the world before the internet. Flipping through encyclopedias for answers, using a phone booth to call home, taking photos with a camera that had film in it, and the list goes on! The world got faster and more connected, which subsequently meant that as humans we became more connected.

Connectivity is about forging bonds that transcend physical distances and differences. In a connected world, you have the opportunity to build meaningful relationships with people from all walks of life. Embrace the tools and opportunities that allow you to connect, whether through technology, shared interests, or community involvement. By nurturing these connections, you create a network of support, inspiration, and mutual growth. Celebrate the richness that connectivity brings to your life.

DEAR UNIVERSE,
I nurture meaningful connectivity, building a supportive and inspiring network that enriches my life.

so be it,
so it is.

25

fondness

FONDNESS IS THE WARMTH AND AFFECTION you feel toward others, places, things, and experiences. It encompasses the simple joys and deep appreciation that make relationships and experiences special. Cultivate fondness by expressing gratitude, sharing kind words, and spending quality time with loved ones and cherished environments. Let your fondness shine through your actions, creating a ripple effect of love and positivity.

By fostering an environment of affection and appreciation, you strengthen your bonds, enrich your experiences, and create lasting memories. Reflect on the people, places, things, and experiences you are fond of the most in your life right now.

DEAR UNIVERSE,
I express fondness and gratitude toward my loved ones, sending out a wave of energy of love and positivity.

so be it,
so it is.

inclusiveness

INCLUSIVENESS IS THE PRACTICE OF EMBRACING diversity and creating a sense of belonging for everyone. When you foster inclusiveness, you honor the unique perspectives and experiences that each person brings. Strive to create spaces where everyone feels valued, respected, and heard. By championing inclusiveness, you build stronger, more vibrant communities.

In 2024, I was invited to Drag Queen Bingo in East Hampton with a group of friends, and it was incredibly fun. People from all walks of life attended, and there was so much laughter, connection, and community. This event was a beautiful example of how inclusiveness can bring people together, making everyone feel cherished, accepted, and loved for who they are.

Inclusiveness works to ensure that no one is left behind, fostering an environment where everyone can thrive. It means actively supporting and uplifting those around us, celebrating their unique qualities, and acknowledging their worth. By doing so, we create a world where everyone feels seen and appreciated.

Celebrate the beauty of diversity and the strength that comes from unity. Let's commit to building communities where love, respect, and acceptance are at the forefront, ensuring that everyone feels they belong.

DEAR UNIVERSE,
I wholeheartedly champion inclusiveness, embracing diversity and creating a sense of belonging for all.

so be it,
so it is.

27

solidarity

SOLIDARITY IS THE STRENGTH THAT ARISES when we stand together in unity and purpose. This is one of the most important fields of energy that we can engage our spirits in. Especially if you are a parent—presenting a united parenting front is crucial in order to raise children to feel a solid foundation.

When you show solidarity, you affirm your commitment to collective well-being and shared goals. Whether it's supporting a cause, lending a hand to someone in need, or standing up for what you believe in, your actions create a powerful force for positive change. Embrace the spirit of solidarity by fostering a sense of community and cooperation. Remember, together we are stronger, and our collective efforts can overcome any challenge.

DEAR UNIVERSE,
I stand in solidarity with those around me, fostering unity and collective strength for positive change.

so be it,
so it is.

soulmate

A TRUE SOULMATE IS NOT JUST a romantic partner; they are a mirror reflecting your deepest truths, a companion on your journey of self-discovery. To identify a true soulmate, look for the one who sees and accepts you for who you are, flaws and all. They bring out your best qualities, encouraging growth, happiness, and self-improvement. With them, you feel an inexplicable connection, as if you've known each other for lifetimes. Communication with a soulmate flows effortlessly; they understand your thoughts and emotions without needing words. In their presence, you find a sense of peace and belonging, as if you've finally come home. A true soulmate challenges you, supports you, and stands by you through life's storms. Together, you share not just love, but a profound partnership built on mutual respect, trust, and unwavering commitment. Your paths align naturally, and your dreams intertwine seamlessly.

Even if it feels like you may never find your soulmate or you have doubts about wanting to find one, remember that the journey of love is unique for everyone. When you find your true soulmate, you don't just feel love; you feel a deep, soul-stirring connection that transcends time and space. This bond is a rare and precious gift that enriches every aspect of your being, and it often arrives when you least expect it. Trust in the timing of your life, and know that this profound connection is worth the wait.

DEAR UNIVERSE,
I cherish the deep connection with my soulmate, nurturing our bond with love, trust, and mutual respect.

so be it,
so it is.

MONTH 3
resilience and strength

On your journey of manifestation and personal growth, developing resilience is key to overcoming life's challenges. This month, we focus on building the inner strength needed to persist toward your goals, dreams, and desires regardless of the obstacles you might face.

Resilience is about growing stronger through each experience and staying committed to your vision. It's the beautiful ability to adapt, remain hopeful, and turn setbacks into opportunities for growth.

REMEMBER: You are a resilient soul, and the Universe will never give you more than you can handle. Trust your journey and embrace the strength within you.

perseverance

WE GRIT OUR TEETH, roll up our sleeves, grin and bear it in order to persevere sometimes, especially during seasons of struggle in our lives. If this is you, right now, please know you are not alone.

Life often presents us with challenges that test our resolve and determination. It's in these moments that perseverance becomes our greatest ally. Perseverance is about staying committed to your dreams and goals, even when the journey feels tough and the path seems unclear. It's about pushing forward, one step at a time, with unwavering faith in your ability to overcome any obstacle.

Remember, each setback is a setup for a comeback. Every hurdle you face is an opportunity to grow stronger and wiser. It's an invitation from the Universe to rise above the limitation, embrace the process, and trust that your efforts will be rewarded.

DEAR UNIVERSE, thank you for giving me the strength to activate the energy of perseverance. I am committed to my dreams and trust that every step I take brings me closer to them.

so be it, so it is.

2

fortitude

IN THE FACE OF ADVERSITY, fortitude is the inner strength that enables you to endure and overcome. It is the steadfastness that keeps you grounded and the resolve that carries you through the toughest times. Fortitude is not about avoiding difficulties but about confronting them with grace and courage.

DEAR UNIVERSE,
I am grateful for the fortitude within me. I face each challenge with strength and resilience, knowing that I can overcome anything.

so be it,
so it is.

Life's challenges are inevitable, but your response to them defines your character. Embrace the trials and tribulations as opportunities to cultivate your inner fortitude.

With fortitude, you can weather any storm and emerge even stronger. Always believe in your ability to endure, and let your inner strength guide you through life's challenges.

Remember, you are capable of far more than you realize. And always remember the phrase: This too shall pass.

bravery

YOU ARE SO MUCH BRAVER THAN you think you are. Bravery is the courage to face fear head-on and take action despite uncertainty. It's about stepping out of your comfort zone and daring to pursue your dreams, even when the outcome is uncertain. Bravery is not the absence of fear, but the triumph over it.

Bravery is about trusting yourself and your abilities, knowing that you have the power to navigate whatever comes your way. Embrace the unknown and take bold steps toward your goals, knowing that each act of bravery brings you closer to living your true potential.

DEAR UNIVERSE, thank you for the bravery within my heart. I face my fears with courage and take bold steps toward my dreams and desires.

so be it, so it is.

You have an inner warrior, capable of remarkable feats. Let them shine through in everything you do, and watch as your life transforms in ways you never thought possible.

Remember, the greatest achievements often require the greatest acts of bravery.

4

resilience

RESILIENCE IS THE ABILITY TO BOUNCE back from life's setbacks and emerge stronger. It's about adapting to change and finding the strength to keep going, no matter what challenges you face. Resilience is your inner reservoir of strength that helps you navigate life's ups and downs with grace and determination.

Life will always present you with obstacles, but your resilience ensures that you can handle anything that comes your way. Embrace each challenge as an opportunity to grow and learn. Trust that every difficulty you overcome builds your resilience, making you more capable and confident.

Your resilience is a testament to your inner strength and your ability to thrive despite adversity. Let it be the guiding force that helps you rise above challenges and continue on your path toward your dreams. Remember, you are stronger than you think, and your resilience will carry you through any storm.

DEAR UNIVERSE,
I am grateful for the resilience within me. I rise above challenges with grace and emerge stronger each time.

so be it,
so it is.

courageous

BEING COURAGEOUS MEANS EMBRACING YOUR FEARS and taking action despite them. It's about having the heart to pursue your dreams and the strength to face whatever comes your way. Courage is the willingness to step into the unknown and trust in your ability to navigate it.

The day I left my first husband back in 2009, I mustered all of the courage I had within me to do so. I had two children, $30,000 worth of debt, and no idea how I was going to support myself. The only thing I knew was that not having the courage to leave was going to cost me so much more than leaving. Once I left, I never looked back, and I'm so proud of the courage I summoned to leap out of my comfort zone and to begin the next chapter of my life.

Remember, courage is not the absence of fear, but the determination to move forward despite it.

DEAR UNIVERSE,
I call upon the energy to be courageous. I embrace my fears and take bold steps toward my dreams with confidence.

so be it,
so it is.

6

tenacity

TENACITY IS THE UNYIELDING DRIVE TO keep pushing forward, no matter how tough the road gets. It's about holding on to your vision with fierce dedication and never giving up, even when the odds seem stacked against you. Your tenacity is what fuels your journey and keeps you moving toward your dreams.

Every challenge you face is a test of your tenacity. Embrace these moments as opportunities to prove to yourself just how resilient and determined you are. When you refuse to give up, you show the world—and yourself—what you're truly capable of.

Remember, the path to success is rarely a straight line. It's filled with twists, turns, and obstacles that will test your resolve. But with tenacity, you can navigate these challenges and continue to move forward. Stay focused on your goals, keep pushing through the tough times, and trust that your tenacity will lead you to success.

DEAR UNIVERSE, thank you for the tenacity within me. I embrace challenges with unwavering determination and push forward toward my dreams.

*so be it,
so it is.*

determination

HAVE YOU EVER SEEN A TODDLER attempt to take their first steps? It's actually quite magnificent. I remember when my daughter Olivia was about thirteen months old and I was making dinner in the kitchen. My children were playing together quietly until my son Thomas said: "She's gonna walk, Mum!"

I turned around and saw this gorgeous little cherub placing one foot in front of the other. She had the most intense look of determination on her face, and it was something I'll never forget.

When you are determined, you refuse to be swayed by setbacks or difficulties. You keep your eyes on the prize and take consistent action toward your goals. Every step you take, no matter how small, brings you closer to your dreams.

DEAR UNIVERSE,
I am grateful for my determination. I pursue my goals with relentless focus and unwavering commitment.

so be it,
so it is.

8

strength

STRENGTH IS NOT JUST ABOUT PHYSICAL power; it's about the inner fortitude that enables you to face life's challenges with grace and resilience. It's the courage to stand tall in the face of adversity and the will to keep moving forward, no matter what.

Your inner strength is a powerful force that can carry you through any storm. Embrace it, nurture it, and let it guide you through life's ups and downs. Each challenge you face is an opportunity to grow stronger and more resilient.

DEAR UNIVERSE, thank you for the strength within me. I face challenges with courage and resilience, knowing I can overcome anything.

so be it, so it is.

Remember, strength comes from within. Make a list of all the ways you've had to exhibit strength in your life to this point in time. What you'll likely see is the map that has made you the beautiful, brilliant, and wise person you are today.

endurance

YOUR ENDURANCE IS A TESTAMENT TO your inner strength and determination. Embrace the journey, and trust that your efforts will be rewarded. Each step you take, no matter how difficult, brings you closer to your dreams.

Remember, success is not a sprint; it's a marathon. It requires patience, persistence, and the willingness to keep pushing forward, even when the road is tough. Stay focused on your goals, maintain your endurance, and trust that you have the strength to see it through.

There's something I like to call eleventh hour manifestation, that just as you're on the brink of giving up, you need to push past the resistance. Your endurance in this phase will help to manifest your success. Whatever you do, always believe beyond what you can see.

DEAR UNIVERSE,
I am grateful for my endurance. I remain steadfast in the pursuit of my goals, knowing my efforts will be rewarded.

so be it,
so it is.

10

steadfast

BEING STEADFAST MEANS STAYING TRUE to your goals and values, no matter what challenges come your way. It's about maintaining your focus and commitment, even (and especially) in the face of adversity. Your steadfastness is a testament to your inner strength and resilience.

When I first started out as an entrepreneur and as a single mother living on welfare, I had to fiercely hold on to my dreams. My steadfast nature helped me to believe that it was possible to keep going and to believe beyond what I could see. I still pinch myself that my life radically changed as much as it did.

Remember, staying steadfast is about holding on to your dreams and values, even when the going gets tough. Stay focused, stay committed, and trust that your steadfast nature will carry you through any challenge.

DEAR UNIVERSE, thank you for the energy to be steadfast. I remain true to my goals and values, no matter what challenges come my way.

so be it, so it is.

robust

FLORENCE SCOVEL SHINN, the author of the 1928 classic Law of Attraction text *The Game of Life and How to Play It*, famously stated that success isn't a secret; it's a system. Indeed, it is a remarkably robust system at its best.

Embracing a robust mindset means cultivating the physical, emotional, and mental fortitude to navigate life's challenges. Nourish your body with healthy habits, your mind with positive thoughts, and your spirit with meaningful connections. When you prioritize your well-being, you become a powerful force capable of overcoming obstacles and thriving in any environment. Embrace the robust energy within you, and let it fuel your journey toward a vibrant and fulfilling life.

DEAR UNIVERSE, I embrace my robust strength, nurturing my body, mind, and spirit to thrive and overcome all challenges.

so be it, so it is.

12

empowerment

MANIFESTING EMPOWERMENT IN MY LIFE HAS been a transformative journey, one that has reshaped my reality and aligned me with my true self. Growing up, I often felt powerless, caught in circumstances that seemed beyond my control. But deep within, I knew there was a spark, a potential waiting to be ignited.

Empowerment is about reclaiming your power and believing in your ability to create the life you desire. It starts with self-awareness and recognizing your innate worth. When you empower yourself, you take control of your destiny, making choices that align with your highest good.

Remember, you have the power within you to achieve greatness and transform your dreams into reality. Stand tall, believe in yourself, and let your light shine.

DEAR UNIVERSE,
I embrace my power and potential for empowerment. I am confidently creating the life I desire and achieving greatness.

so be it,
so it is.

valor

VALOR IS NOT THE ABSENCE OF FEAR, but the strength to face it with unwavering courage.

It is the inner resolve to stand up for what you believe in, even when it's difficult. Embrace your valor by acknowledging your fears and pushing past them. Each challenge you overcome strengthens your spirit and builds your beautiful character. Let your courage inspire others and create a ripple effect of bravery and resilience. Stand firm in your convictions and approach life with a warrior's heart.

DEAR UNIVERSE,
I embody valor, courageously facing challenges and standing firm in my convictions with a warrior's heart.

so be it,
so it is.

14

fearlessness

WHEN YOU CHOOSE TO BE FEARLESS, you step out of your comfort zone (where the magic happens) and embrace the unknown with confidence and curiosity.

One significant example of my fearlessness was when I moved from Australia to the United States. This bold step required leaving behind familiar surroundings and starting anew, symbolizing my commitment to growth and my willingness to take risks in pursuit of my dreams.

Launching my business was another fearless act. Building a brand and a following in the highly competitive field of manifestation and self-help required a deep belief in my vision and the courage to stand out. I not only created a successful business but also became a voice of inspiration for millions, sharing my journey and insights through books, courses, and public speaking.

DEAR UNIVERSE, may I embrace fearlessness, stepping boldly into the unknown with confidence and curiosity, knowing I am supported.

so be it, so it is.

Trust in your abilities and the support of the Universe. Every step you take in faith strengthens your resolve and opens new doors of opportunity. Let your fearlessness guide you to new heights and adventures, showing you just how capable you are.

boldness

MAKE IT YOUR MISSION TO BE a little more bold and daring if you can. Being bold is about living authentically and unapologetically. Embrace being bold by expressing your true self, pursuing your passions, and daring to dream big. When you act with boldness, you inspire others to do the same, creating a ripple effect of courage and innovation. Stand out, take charge, and let your bold spirit lead the way to a life of purpose and fulfillment. Try making a bold statement on social media and sharing it without fear of judgment.

As the saying goes: "Dance like no one is watching."

DEAR UNIVERSE, may I embrace more boldness in my life, living authentically and daring to take risks in pursuit of my true desires.

so be it, so it is.

grit

YOU KNOW THE ROAD AHEAD IS TOUGH, the path steep and often lonely. Yet, here you are, ready to face it all with unwavering determination. Remember, true grit isn't just about pushing through obstacles; it's about embracing them as part of your journey. It's the resilience in your heart and the steadfastness of your spirit that make you unbreakable. You, armed with the courage to stand back up every time life tries to knock you down, are a force to be reckoned with. Let each setback teach you and every challenge refine you.

DEAR UNIVERSE, grant me the strength to persevere, the courage to endure, and the wisdom to grow from my challenges with grit and grace.

so be it, so it is.

You are not just surviving; you are thriving, growing stronger with every step you take.

unyielding

IMAGINE YOURSELF AS A MIGHTY OAK TREE, deeply rooted and firmly planted in the earth. Even when storms rage, you remain anchored, unyielding in your essence. Life's tempests cannot sway you because your heart is resolved and your purpose clear.

Embrace this unyielding spirit within you. Let it guide you through trials and tribulations, knowing that what truly matters cannot be shaken.

Stand firm in your beliefs and values; let them be the compass that steers you through the murkiest waters. You are built not just to withstand but to rise above it.

DEAR UNIVERSE, empower me to stand firm in my convictions, unyielding in adversity, strong in my resolve.

so be it, so it is.

unflappable

IN A WORLD OFTEN CHARACTERIZED BY TURBULENCE, especially in these modern times, being unflappable is a rare and powerful trait. You possess an inner calm, a core of tranquility amid the chaos. In every situation, let your inner serenity prevail. When others are swept up by waves of panic, you stand composed, your peace unbroken.

This tranquility is your beautiful armor and your calm demeanor, your shield. Let this inner peace guide your actions and soothe those around you. In calmness, there is great strength—embrace it, and you become invincible.

DEAR UNIVERSE, bless me with an unflappable tranquil heart and a serene mind that remains composed in every challenge.

so be it, so it is.

dignified

YOU DESERVE DIGNITY IN ALL SITUATIONS that life presents you with. Dignity is the cloak you wear, woven from the fabric of your self-respect and grace. Carry yourself with the poise of one who knows their worth and treats themselves and others with profound respect. In a world that often forgets the value of integrity, let yours be the light that guides the way.

It involves conducting oneself with integrity, compassion, and a deep sense of self-respect. Living with dignity means staying true to one's values, treating others with kindness and fairness, and navigating life's challenges with grace and poise. By embracing dignity, we create a foundation for meaningful relationships and a life of purpose.

DEAR UNIVERSE, let me always act in a dignified manner, respect myself fully, and inspire respect in others.

so be it, so it is.

20

assertive

"THAT'S NOT GOING TO HAPPEN," I firmly responded when a strange drunk man in the Vegas elevator asked if I would consider coming back to his hotel room. With seven floors to go before I could exit, I had to muster the energy to confront his blatant overstep of boundaries. It's incredibly important to speak your truth, even when your voice shakes, in situations where people cross the line in the most confronting ways. You have to be assertive. And if you are a parent, you must always lead by example and teach your children to use their words to set strong boundaries that they do not allow to be crossed.

Being assertive is your declaration of self-respect and your testament to personal strength. It is the voice that says, "I am here, I matter." Let this voice be heard in all your interactions. Speak your truth clearly and confidently without overshadowing others. Assertiveness isn't about dominance; it's about honest expression and mutual respect. It's about setting boundaries and respecting those of others. Embrace your assertive spirit and watch as it transforms your relationships and fortifies your inner strength.

DEAR UNIVERSE, empower me to express myself confidently and respectfully in an empowering and assertive way.

so be it, so it is.

unstoppable

THERE HAVE BEEN TIMES IN MY LIFE, especially when working on creative projects, when I affirm that I can't stop and I won't stop. It helps to harness your inner strength and determination to overcome any obstacle. It's about having a relentless spirit and an unshakable belief in your ability to achieve your dreams.

When you face challenges, remember that you have the power to keep moving forward, no matter what. Embrace your unstoppable nature by staying focused on your goals and taking consistent action. With perseverance and resilience, you can turn your vision into reality and achieve greatness.

DEAR UNIVERSE,
I am unstoppable, harnessing my inner strength and determination to achieve my dreams and overcome any obstacle.

so be it,
so it is.

22

vigorous

LIVING A VIGOROUS LIFE MEANS EMBRACING ENERGY, vitality, and enthusiasm in all that you do. It's about approaching each day with zest and a positive attitude, ready to tackle whatever comes your way.

Cultivate vigor by nurturing your body through exercise, nourishing your mind with learning, and feeding your spirit with joy and purpose.

DEAR UNIVERSE,
I embrace vigorous energy, vitality, and enthusiasm in all that I do.

so be it,
so it is.

When you live vigorously, you attract opportunities and inspire others with your radiant energy. Embrace the vibrancy within you and let it infuse every aspect of your life.

resourceful

WHEN I WAS A SINGLE MOTHER living on welfare in Australia, I would have to be incredibly resourceful to make ends meet. I would add water to the ketchup bottle to make it last a little longer, I would clip coupons, I would shop at secondhand stores, and always be prepared to think creatively in order to provide for my children.

Being resourceful means creatively solving problems and making the most of what you have. It's about leveraging your skills, knowledge, and networks to find innovative solutions and opportunities. When you are resourceful, you see possibilities where others see limitations. Embrace your resourcefulness by trusting in your abilities and thinking outside the box. With a resourceful mindset, you can navigate challenges with ease, maximize your potential, and achieve your goals in remarkable ways.

DEAR UNIVERSE,
I am resourceful, creatively solving problems and making the most of my skills and opportunities.

so be it,
so it is.

24

dauntless

BEING DAUNTLESS MEANS HAVING THE COURAGE to face fears and challenges head-on, without hesitation. It's about possessing a fearless spirit and an unwavering resolve to pursue your dreams. When you are dauntless, you embrace uncertainty and rise above adversity with confidence.

Embrace your dauntless nature by believing in yourself and taking bold steps toward your goals. With courage and determination, you can overcome any obstacle and live a life of boundless possibilities.

DEAR UNIVERSE,
I am dauntless, facing fears and challenges with unwavering courage and confidence.

so be it,
so it is.

gallant

BEING GALLANT MEANS EMBODYING BRAVERY, chivalry, and honor in all your actions, and it's not just reserved for stereotypical masculine energy. It's about being a decent human being. For instance, I open the door for people regardless of gender because it's a gallant and kind thing to do. I also love it when other people take initiative and help out.

Being gallant is about facing challenges with courage and treating others with respect and kindness. When you act gallantly, you inspire those around you and create a positive impact in your community. Embrace your inner hero by standing up for what is right, offering help where needed, and maintaining your integrity. Let your gallant spirit shine through, showing the world your unwavering commitment to living with valor and grace. What can you do to kindly assist someone today?

DEAR UNIVERSE,
I embrace my gallant spirit, facing challenges with bravery and treating others with honor and respect.

so be it,
so it is.

26

resolute

WE ALL SPEAK OF RESOLUTIONS as the clock strikes midnight on New Year's Eve each year—however, do you truly align with the energy of being resolute?

Being resolute means having a firm determination to achieve your goals and stay true to your values, no matter the obstacles. It's about having a clear vision and the tenacity to see it through to the end. When you are resolute, you remain steadfast in your purpose, undeterred by setbacks. Embrace your resolute nature by setting clear intentions and taking consistent, deliberate actions, and not just when it is the beginning of the year. Your unwavering determination will guide you to success and fulfillment and carry you through any season in life.

DEAR UNIVERSE,
I am resolute in my purpose, steadfastly pursuing my goals with unwavering determination.

so be it,
so it is.

audacious

WHEN I WAS NINETEEN, IN 1999, I worked in a lingerie store called Audacity as a retail assistant. Men would come in around Valentine's Day and not know the bra size of their spouse. And to make matters worse, they would use my chest as a visual benchmark to state that their wife was either larger or smaller than me! It was a short-lived place of employment for me and, ironically, the boss didn't understand why I had the audacity to leave after only a few short weeks.

Being audacious means having the boldness to take risks and pursue your dreams fearlessly. It's about stepping out of your comfort zone and daring to achieve the extraordinary. When you embrace audacity, you ignite your potential and open doors to new opportunities. Let your audacious spirit guide you to dream big and act courageously. Trust in your ability to overcome challenges and make your mark on the world with your fearless pursuit of greatness.

DEAR UNIVERSE,
I embrace my audacious spirit, boldly pursuing my dreams and taking courageous risks.

so be it,
so it is.

28

stalwart

BEING STALWART MEANS BEING DEPENDABLE, loyal, and unwavering in your commitment. It's about standing firm in your beliefs and supporting others with steadfast dedication.

When you are stalwart, you provide strength and stability to those around you. Embrace your steadfast nature by staying true to your principles and being a reliable source of support for others. Your unwavering loyalty and dependability will build lasting trust and inspire those you encounter. What are some of the principles that you stand firm in? List them out as your energetic North Star to stand by no matter what.

DEAR UNIVERSE,
I am stalwart and unwavering, standing firm in my beliefs and providing dependable support to others.

*so be it,
so it is.*

invincible

TO PUT IT IN THE LYRICS OF A JOHN MAYER SONG: "I am invincible as long as I am alive."

We're human, and the more we remember that the Universe will never give us more than we can handle, it manifests the powerful energy of invincibility.

Being invincible means having an unbreakable spirit and the belief that you can overcome any challenge. It's about embracing your inner strength and resilience, knowing that nothing can defeat you. When you see yourself as invincible, you approach life with confidence and determination. Let your invincible nature guide you to face difficulties head-on and emerge stronger. Trust in your ability to navigate any obstacle and achieve greatness with your indomitable spirit.

DEAR UNIVERSE,
I am invincible, facing challenges with unbreakable strength and confidence, knowing I can overcome anything.

so be it,
so it is.

30

unwavering

IN EARLY 2020, I LIVED ON less than ten dollars per day to feed myself and my children. I was a single mother, in massive debt and struggling to make ends meet. My commitment to getting through each day with strength for the sake of my children was unwavering. I had one job to do, and that was to stay strong so they didn't feel fearful or unprotected.

Being unwavering means staying steadfast and committed to your goals and values, no matter the circumstances. It's about having a clear focus and remaining resolute in the face of adversity. When you are unwavering, you demonstrate remarkable perseverance and dedication. Embrace your unwavering spirit by staying true to your path and not letting external pressures sway you. Your steadfast commitment will lead you to accomplish your dreams and inspire others along the way.

DEAR UNIVERSE,
I am unwavering in my commitment, steadfastly pursuing my goals and staying true to my values.

so be it,
so it is.

triumphant

EVERY MOMENT CAN BE A CELEBRATION, filled with the electrifying energy of knowing you've overcome obstacles and emerged victorious. Let the dazzling display of your triumph inspire you to reach for even greater heights. You should be so proud of how far you've come in your life.

Being triumphant is about acknowledging your achievements and the hard work that made them possible. When you embrace a triumphant mindset, you inspire yourself and others to reach new heights. Celebrate your triumphs with gratitude and pride, and use them as fuel to pursue even greater goals. Let your spirit of triumph guide you to continuous growth and success.

DEAR UNIVERSE,
I celebrate being triumphant with gratitude and pride, using them as fuel for even greater success.

so be it,
so it is.

MONTH 4

mindfulness and presence

Embracing mindfulness and being present in the moment are essential for your manifestation journey. This month, we focus on cultivating awareness and fully engaging in your experiences with a sense of activating the magic of the present moment.

Mindfulness helps you connect with your true self, quieting the mind and fostering inner peace. By being present, you enhance your ability to manifest your desires, as you are fully aligned with the here and now.

REMEMBER: Presence is the gateway to your highest potential. Stay mindful, cherish each moment, and watch as your manifestations unfold with clarity and ease.

aware

ONE DAY YOU WILL BECOME AWARE of the first steps toward transformation in any given moment. In the hustle of daily life, it's so easy to overlook the beauty and opportunities that surround you. When you truly awaken to the details of your heart and your inner world, you begin to see the miracles that are constantly unfolding.

Awareness opens the door to understanding, and often precedes great and wonderful change. Notice the subtle colors of the sky, the soul-stirring sound of laughter, and the feelings within your heart. This heightened awareness connects you to the present moment and all the possibilities it holds.

DEAR UNIVERSE,
I am open to and aware of the beauty and opportunities that surround me each day. I embrace every moment with clarity and gratitude.

so be it,
so it is.

2

present

WHEN MY TWO OLDEST CHILDREN WERE LITTLE, I remember writing a statement for my future self in my journal. It read: "Remember to celebrate that you were present for your children even in the tiniest moments. The present moment is all you ever have, they grow so fast." And they did.

Life is a collection of moments, each one precious and unique. By being fully present, you honor the now and create a deeper connection with yourself and others. Let go of the past and release the future, immersing yourself in the richness of this moment. Whether you're sharing a conversation, savoring a meal, or simply breathing, being present transforms ordinary experiences into extraordinary ones. Embrace the power of now, and let it guide you to a more fulfilled and joyful life.

DEAR UNIVERSE,
I commit to being fully present in each moment, embracing the now with my whole heart and mind. I honor the gift of today.

*so be it,
so it is.*

mindful

CALL IN THE ENERGY OF BEING more mindful today. Mindfulness is the practice of paying attention to your thoughts, feelings, and actions without judgment. It allows you to live with intention and purpose. When you are mindful, you create space to respond rather than react, to choose peace over chaos, and to appreciate the simple joys of life.

Start each day with a mindful breath, and carry that awareness with you. As you cultivate mindfulness, you will find greater balance, harmony, and contentment in all that you do. Meditation is also the best way to connect with the Universe within—this helps you to become more mindful with the choices you make on a day-to-day basis.

DEAR UNIVERSE,
I choose to live in a mindful way, embracing each thought, feeling, and action with intention and purpose. I am at peace and in harmony.

so be it, so it is.

4

conscious

LIVING A CONSCIOUS LIFE MEANS MAKING deliberate choices that align with your true self and highest good. It requires you to awaken from autopilot mode and actively participate in your own journey.

DEAR UNIVERSE,
I choose to be as conscious as possibile, making deliberate decisions that align with my highest good and true self. I am empowered and intentional.

so be it,
so it is.

When you are conscious, you are in tune with your values, desires, and the impact of your actions. This awareness empowers you to create a life that reflects your deepest truths. Embrace your power to make conscious choices, and watch as your life transforms in beautiful and unexpected ways.

focused

FOCUS IS THE BRIDGE BETWEEN DREAMS AND REALITY. It requires you to channel your energy and attention toward what truly matters. By eliminating distractions and homing in on your goals, you create a powerful momentum that propels you forward. Stay committed to your vision, and trust in your ability to achieve it.

With focus, you can turn your aspirations into tangible outcomes. Embrace this discipline, and let it guide you to your fullest potential. What can you bring focus to today that will help you feel more inspired about your future?

DEAR UNIVERSE,
I dedicate my focused energy to my highest goals and dreams, channeling my intentions toward creating my desired reality. I am driven and committed.

so be it,
so it is.

6

centered

WHEN YOU ARE CENTERED, you are anchored in your true self, unaffected by external chaos. It's a beautiful feeling. Take time each day to connect with your inner calm through meditation, deep breathing, or simply being still.

DEAR UNIVERSE,
I remain centered and calm amid life's chaos, deeply rooted in my true self and inner peace.

so be it,
so it is.

This practice helps you navigate life's challenges with grace and resilience. By staying centered, you maintain a steady course, no matter the storms that come your way. Embrace your inner sanctuary and let it be your guiding light.

clarity

CLARITY IS A GIFT THAT ILLUMINATES your path and dispels confusion. It allows you to see your goals, values, and dreams in an illuminated new light. When you manifest clarity, decision-making becomes effortless, and your actions are aligned with your highest purpose. Take time to clear the mental clutter through reflection, journaling, or speaking with trusted friends. As you gain clarity, you step into your power, making choices that resonate with your true desires and aspirations.

For me, clarity often is a deep knowing of the path forward. That all options have been weighed up and it's time to take a leap of faith. Try it for yourself and see what manifests from a beautiful space of clarity.

DEAR UNIVERSE,
I embrace clarity, seeing my path and purpose with precision and confidence. My mind and heart are clear and aligned.

so be it, so it is.

perceptive

HAVE YOU EVER NOTICED THE SLIGHTEST shift in energy just by staring into someone's eyes? The way the tiniest micro-change shows you that their thoughts just took a different direction? Perception lives in the subtleties of life. In fact, your perception shapes your reality. Being perceptive means tuning in to the subtle cues and underlying truths that others might miss. It involves listening with empathy, observing with curiosity, and understanding with great depth. This heightened awareness allows you to connect more deeply with others and navigate complex situations with insight and wisdom.

I invite you to remember today to trust that your keen senses will guide you toward greater understanding and meaningful connections. Being perceptive could even keep you safe from harm.

DEAR UNIVERSE,
I trust my perceptive abilities to see beyond the surface, understanding deeply and connecting profoundly.

*so be it,
so it is.*

intuition

ONE SUMMER I VISITED SEDONA, ARIZONA. It's known for the beautiful red rock formations and spiritual vortexes. A spiritual vortex is a location on Earth believed to have a concentrated energy field that can enhance meditation, healing, and spiritual awakening. The energy in this place is truly magnificent. However, while I was hiking, I got bitten by mosquitoes, which left me with well over a hundred bites all over my legs. The itching was horrendous. As the welts healed, I noticed a small patch of skin on the back of my calf that I'd never noticed before. My intuition told me to go and get it checked out. After a small biopsy, I was told it was a basal cell carcinoma. Had I not been bitten by those mosquitoes (as annoying as they were), I would not have followed my intuition to get checked out.

Your intuition is your superpower—never forget that. Your intuition is always leading you toward your highest good and keeping you safe. Trusting your intuition means listening to that quiet, inner voice and following its wisdom, even when it defies logic. This inner knowing is a direct line to your true self and the Universe's guidance. Strengthen your intuition by practicing mindfulness, paying attention to your feelings, and embracing your instincts. As you honor your intuition, you will find that it leads you to opportunities, people, and experiences that resonate with your soul's purpose.

DEAR UNIVERSE,
I honor and trust my intuition, allowing it to guide me toward my highest good and true path.

so be it,
so it is.

10

attentive

I HOPE YOU GET TO EXPERIENCE the magic of someone being attentive to you in ways that make you feel valued, loved, and seen. Being attentive is about giving your full focus and presence to the moment at hand. It's about listening deeply, observing keenly, and engaging fully with life. This attentiveness enriches your experiences, deepens your relationships, and enhances your personal growth. Practice being attentive by eliminating distractions, focusing on one task at a time, and truly being present with those around you.

As you cultivate attentiveness, you will discover a richer, more fulfilling way of living.

DEAR UNIVERSE,
I am fully attentive to each moment, giving my focus and presence to what truly matters.

so be it,
so it is.

observant

IMAGINE YOURSELF AS A WATCHFUL EAGLE soaring high above the landscape. From this vantage point, you can see the intricate details of the world below—the subtle movements of animals, the patterns of rivers winding through the earth, the way the sunlight dances on the leaves. As you become more observant, you notice the beauty and complexity in every moment, gaining a deeper appreciation for life.

This heightened awareness allows you to navigate your journey with clarity and insight, recognizing opportunities and understanding the subtle cues around you. Embrace your inner eagle, and let your observant nature guide you.

DEAR UNIVERSE,
I embrace my observant nature, noticing the beauty and complexity in every moment.

so be it,
so it is.

12

composed

WHEN I MOVED TO SWEDEN IN MY TWENTIES, the first leg of the flight, from Australia to Malaysia, was a nightmare. I tried to remain composed, but my three-year-old son, Thomas, screamed his head off the entire way. I got scowls from other passengers, and nothing would soothe Thomas from the pressure he was obviously feeling in his tiny ears. Inside, I was screaming too. Think of the times in your own life that have called for great composure and how well you navigated it.

Visualize yourself as a strong, deeply rooted tree. Despite fierce winds or heavy rains, you remain grounded and composed. Your branches may sway, but your core stands unmoved, drawing strength from deep roots, a pillar of stability in all seasons.

DEAR UNIVERSE,
I embrace my inner calm, remaining composed and steady through all of life's challenges.

*so be it,
so it is.*

reflective

TAKE A MOMENT TO SIT QUIETLY and reflect on your journey. Picture your life as a river, flowing smoothly over time. Each bend in the river represents a significant moment, each ripple a lesson learned. By reflecting on these moments, you gain a deeper understanding of your growth and the wisdom you have accumulated. This practice of reflection helps you to appreciate how far you've come and to set a clear direction for the future.

Let the flow of the river remind you that every experience, good or bad, contributes to your overall journey.

DEAR UNIVERSE,
I embrace my life with reflective energy, gaining clarity and insight into my journey and growth.

so be it,
so it is.

14

tranquil

AMID THE NOISE AND DEMANDS OF LIFE, seek out tranquility. Find those serene spaces where you can reconnect with your inner peace. Whether it's a quiet corner of your home, a peaceful walk in nature, or a moment of meditation, these tranquil pauses are essential for your well-being.

DEAR UNIVERSE,
I embrace being tranquil, finding peace and balance in my mind and body.

so be it,
so it is.

In tranquility, your mind and spirit find rest, your creativity flows, and your energy rejuvenates. Embrace these moments of calm as a sacred practice, nurturing your soul and restoring balance in your life.

identity

DO YOU KNOW AND REMEMBER WHO YOU TRULY ARE? As I mentioned in the introduction, I woke up one day and knew that I needed to put down the identity that kept me in the role of a people pleaser. Assuming a new identity is about choice.

Think of yourself as a unique star shining brightly in the vast night sky. Your identity is your light, formed by your experiences, values, and dreams. Embrace who you are, with all your strengths and imperfections, knowing that your unique light contributes to the beauty of the Universe. As you journey through life, stay true to your core, honoring your authentic self. Let your identity shine brightly, guiding you and inspiring others. Just as the stars create a beautiful tapestry in the sky, your individuality adds richness and depth to the world. Who will you be today?

DEAR UNIVERSE,
I embrace my true identity, standing tall and proud, confident in who I am.

*so be it,
so it is.*

16

peacefulness

"PEACE COMES FROM WITHIN. Do not seek it without." —Buddha

Imagine a serene lake at dawn, its surface smooth and undisturbed, reflecting the sky's gentle hues. This is the essence of peacefulness.

DEAR UNIVERSE, guide me to embrace peacefulness, allowing my mind and heart to find harmony in every moment.

so be it, so it is.

As you navigate life's turbulence, seek to embody this calm state. Allow your thoughts to settle and your emotions to find harmony. Create spaces in your day for quiet reflection, gentle breathing, and gratitude. By fostering peacefulness within, you not only enhance your own well-being but also radiate tranquility to those around you. Peacefulness is a powerful gift that transforms chaos into clarity and tension into tranquility.

stillness

STILLNESS HOLDS THE MAGIC OF MANIFESTATION. Your awareness of inner stillness—tuning in to your energy and emotions—becomes the most powerful connection point with the Universe.

In a world that moves at a relentless pace, finding stillness is a precious refuge. Close your eyes and imagine yourself in a quiet forest, where the only sounds are the whispers of leaves and the soft rustle of the breeze. This stillness is your sanctuary. It's in these moments of silence that you connect with your deepest self, accessing profound wisdom and inner strength. Embrace stillness as a daily practice, letting it ground you and restore your spirit.

DEAR UNIVERSE, help me to find and embrace stillness, connecting with my inner wisdom and strength.

so be it, so it is.

18

calmness

LIFE'S STORMS MAY RAGE AROUND YOU, but within you lies an ocean of calmness. I picture the Montauk Point Lighthouse, standing strong amid crashing waves, its light unwavering. Located at the easternmost point of Long Island, Montauk is often referred to as "The End" because it marks the farthest point of New York on the coast. Surrounded by the vast Atlantic Ocean, this lighthouse symbolizes resilience and calm in tumultuous waters.

DEAR UNIVERSE, help me to cultivate calmness within, standing strong and serene amid life's storms.

so be it, so it is.

When you cultivate calmness, you become a beacon of stability and serenity. Practice deep breathing, mindfulness, and self-compassion to anchor yourself in this calmness. This inner peace empowers you to face challenges with clarity and grace, ensuring that your light continues to shine bright regardless of external circumstances.

insightful

YOUR JOURNEY IS ILLUMINATED BY MOMENTS of insight. Embrace these flashes of understanding as they guide you toward deeper knowledge and clarity. Like a lantern lighting your path in the dark, insights reveal truths that may have been hidden. Cultivate an open mind and a curious heart, ready to receive wisdom from both expected and unexpected sources.

By being insightful, you transform experiences into learning opportunities and challenges into stepping stones for growth.

DEAR UNIVERSE, grant me the ability to be insightful, recognizing and embracing wisdom from all experiences.

so be it, so it is.

20

grounded

FOR MOST OF MY LIFE, I've experienced some level of anxiety. After 2020, as I embarked on my emotional healing journey, I started having severe panic attacks. One of the few things that helped during these struggles was placing my bare feet on the earth. Known as "grounding," this practice is tremendously effective in calming the central nervous system.

DEAR UNIVERSE, help me stay grounded, connected to my true self and the present moment with resilience and grace.

so be it, so it is.

Feel the earth beneath your feet, steady and strong. This is what it means to be grounded. No matter how high your dreams soar, staying grounded ensures you remain connected to your true self and the present moment. Engage in practices that anchor you, such as walking in nature, meditating, or practicing mindfulness. Grounding keeps you centered and balanced, allowing you to navigate life's challenges with resilience and grace.

21

enlightened

TO BE ENLIGHTENED IS TO SEE beyond the ordinary, to understand the deeper truths of existence. Imagine a vast sky, filled with countless stars, each one a beacon of light and knowledge. Your journey toward enlightenment is illuminated by these stars of wisdom and understanding. Embrace the path of continuous learning and spiritual growth, allowing each experience to expand your consciousness. Enlightenment is not a destination but a journey of perpetual discovery and transformation.

Enlightenment is not about transcending the world, but about deeply embracing it with wisdom and compassion, seeing the interconnectedness of all things and the profound truth of our shared existence.

DEAR UNIVERSE, guide me toward enlightenment, expanding my consciousness and embracing continuous learning and growth.

so be it,
so it is.

22

receptive

THE MOST OFTEN OVERLOOKED ELEMENT IN manifestation is that your capacity to receive impacts what you allow yourself to attract into your life.

Imagine yourself as an open field, ready to receive the gentle rain that nourishes the earth. Being receptive means allowing the Universe's gifts and wisdom to flow into your life. Open your heart and mind to new experiences, ideas, and opportunities. Embrace the unknown with curiosity and trust, knowing that every encounter has the potential to bring growth and insight. By being receptive, you create a space where miracles can manifest, and your life can be enriched in unexpected and beautiful ways.

DEAR UNIVERSE, help me remain open and receptive to your gifts and wisdom, allowing miracles to manifest in my life.

so be it, so it is.

thoughtful

THOUGHTFULNESS IS A POWERFUL PRACTICE THAT enriches your relationships and personal growth. Take a moment to consider the needs and feelings of others, and act with kindness and empathy. Thoughtful actions, whether small or grand, create ripples of positivity that touch the lives of many.

Additionally, being thoughtful toward yourself—acknowledging your needs and treating yourself with compassion—fosters inner peace and well-being. Cultivate thoughtfulness in every interaction, and watch how it transforms your world.

DEAR UNIVERSE, guide me to be thoughtful in all my actions, spreading kindness and empathy to myself and others.

so be it, so it is.

24

contemplative

IN THE STILLNESS OF CONTEMPLATION, you find profound wisdom and clarity. Set aside time each day to reflect on your thoughts, feelings, and experiences.

Contemplation allows you to understand the deeper meanings behind your actions and decisions. It's a journey inward that illuminates your path forward.

By engaging in contemplative practices such as journaling, meditation, or quiet reflection, you gain insights that help you navigate life with purpose and intention.

DEAR UNIVERSE, lead me to a contemplative state, where I can find wisdom and clarity within.

so be it, so it is.

harmonious

IMAGINE A BEAUTIFUL SYMPHONY, EACH INSTRUMENT playing in perfect harmony. This is what it means to live a harmonious life. Strive for balance in all areas—work, relationships, and personal well-being.

When you create harmony within yourself, it naturally extends to your surroundings, fostering peaceful and positive interactions. Embrace practices that promote balance, such as mindfulness, self-care, and open communication. A harmonious life is one of joy, connection, and inner peace.

DEAR UNIVERSE, help me create and maintain harmonious energy in all aspects of my life, fostering peace and balance.

so be it, so it is.

26

introspective

INTROSPECTION IS A POWERFUL TOOL FOR personal growth. Take time to look within, exploring your thoughts, emotions, and motivations. By understanding yourself more deeply, you can align your actions with your true values and desires. Introspection helps you recognize patterns, heal old wounds, and embrace your authentic self. Try engaging in practices such as creative writing, breathwork, or gentle nature strolls to foster self-reflection. This inward journey is the key to unlocking your full potential.

DEAR UNIVERSE, guide me in my introspective journey, helping me understand and embrace my true self.

*so be it,
so it is.*

meditative

WHEN I FIRST STARTED PRACTICING MEDITATION over twenty-five years ago, it opened my world to the awareness of energy and vibration. Meditation is a sanctuary for your soul, a place where you can find peace and clarity. By practicing meditation, you quiet the noise of the outside world and connect with your inner self. This practice enhances your awareness, reduces stress, and fosters a deep sense of calm.

DEAR UNIVERSE, help me embrace meditative energy, finding peace and clarity within its practice.

so be it, so it is.

Make meditation a part of your daily routine (like you are by reading this book), and discover the profound benefits it brings to your mental, emotional, and spiritual well-being.

isness

THERE'S A POWERFUL POPULAR PHRASE THAT people tend to use: "It is what it is." It actually helps you to stop arguing with reality.

Embrace the concept of "isness"—the art of being fully present in the here and now. Imagine yourself sitting by a tranquil river, feeling the gentle flow of water as it moves past you. There is no past or future, only this moment. Isness invites you to let go of worries and distractions, grounding yourself in the present. By doing so, you find peace and clarity, allowing life to unfold naturally. Embrace each moment with openness and acceptance, and discover the profound beauty of simply being.

DEAR UNIVERSE, guide me to embrace the present moment, finding peace and clarity in the isness of this beautiful now moment.

so be it,
so it is.

creativity

FOR ME THERE IS NOTHING MORE exciting than the promise of a blank page when it comes to the creative writing process. There is infinite potential to create worlds, open hearts and minds, and even save lives. We are only limited by our imaginations when it comes to creativity.

Creativity is the spark that ignites your soul and brings your dreams to life. Visualize a blank canvas, waiting for the vibrant colors of your imagination to bring it to life. Whether through art, writing, problem-solving, or innovation, your creativity is limitless. Allow yourself the freedom to explore and express your unique ideas. When you tap into your creative potential, you connect with your true self and bring joy and inspiration to the world.

DEAR UNIVERSE, help me unleash my creativity, expressing my unique ideas with joy and inspiration.

so be it, so it is.

30

musical

MUSIC CAN BRING AN INCREDIBLE AMOUNT of presence and mindfulness into your life. Whether you sing, play an instrument, dance, or even love listening to music—it's an access point to the Universe.

DEAR UNIVERSE, guide me to embrace the musical nature of life, finding my unique voice and harmony.

so be it, so it is.

Think of the music that resonates with your soul the most—this is the key to raising your vibration.

You see life as a symphony, and you are the composer of your own melody. Embrace the musicality of life by tuning in to its rhythms and finding your unique voice.

MONTH 5

self-love and acceptance

Self-love is the cornerstone of personal growth. This month is for your beautiful heart as we delve into the practice of embracing and accepting ourselves fully, promoting confidence and self-compassion and devotion to the Divine.

Cultivating self-love enables you to pursue your dreams without self-imposed limitations. By nurturing acceptance, you release the need for external validation and focus on your intrinsic worth.

REMEMBER: Self-love is the foundation of your journey. Embrace who you are, practice compassion, and watch as your self-belief propels you toward your dreams and desires.

self-compassion

EMBRACING SELF-COMPASSION IS THE FIRST STEP toward healing and personal growth, allowing us to nurture our inner selves with the kindness and understanding we readily offer others. I'd had a rough few months in June 2024, beyond what I was capable of processing emotionally. My marriage had fallen apart, and I was now solely responsible for running the business and the brand by myself for the first time in a decade. I decided to book myself into an oceanside resort to write by the beach. Two marriages biting the dust in my past, I realized I am not defined by my mistakes or shortcomings. It's an invitation from the Universe to practice self-compassion.

DEAR UNIVERSE,
I embrace my imperfections with kindness and understanding. I am worthy of self-compassion and all good things.

so be it,
so it is.

Embrace your humanity and treat yourself with the same kindness you'd offer a dear friend. When you stumble, pause and acknowledge your pain without judgment. Your struggles don't diminish your worth; they're part of your journey. Remember, every person you admire has faced their own battles and moments of doubt. You're no different. Be gentle with yourself as you navigate life's challenges.

self-acceptance

YOU ARE A MASTERPIECE IN PROGRESS, a beautiful blend of strengths and flaws. Imagine standing before a stunning ornate mirror, truly seeing yourself without filters or judgment. That person staring back at you is worthy of acceptance, just as they are. Your quirks, your scars, your unique perspective—they all contribute to the tapestry of who you are. Stop fighting against yourself and start embracing every facet of your being.

Release the need for perfection and allow yourself to simply be. You are not a problem to be fixed, but a person to be loved and understood. Acceptance doesn't mean giving up on growth; it means loving yourself through the process. Let go of the "should haves" and "if onlys." You are here, now, exactly as you're meant to be. Celebrate your authenticity and watch as the world responds to your genuine self.

DEAR UNIVERSE,
I practice self-acceptance fully, embracing all aspects of who I am. My authentic self shines brightly, free from judgment or doubt.

so be it,
so it is.

DAY

3

self-worth

LIKE ME, FOLLOW ME, CHOOSE ME. Many have gotten caught up in the overpowerful noise of social media to find a new method for self-worth to be chipped away at. Your worth is not determined by external validation or accomplishments. It's an inherent quality, as constant as your heartbeat. You don't need to prove your value to anyone—not even yourself. Your mere existence is a miracle, a unique constellation of experiences, thoughts, and potential.

Recognize the power within you to create, to love, to impact the world in ways both big and small. Your worth isn't tied to your productivity or your possessions. It's not diminished by your struggles or elevated by your successes. It simply is. Unshakeable. Immeasurable. Infinite. Embrace this truth and let it guide your actions and decisions. Stand tall in the knowledge that you are worthy, simply because you are you.

DEAR UNIVERSE, my self-worth is intrinsic and unchanging. I recognize my inherent value in every moment, independent of external circumstances.

so be it, so it is.

self-esteem

PICTURE A STURDY OAK TREE, its roots deep in the earth, its branches reaching for the sky with confidence and clarity. This is you—grounded in your values, yet always growing. Your self-esteem is the foundation from which you interact with the world. It's not about being better than others; it's about recognizing your own unique light. Celebrate your victories, no matter how small. Acknowledge your strengths and the challenges you've overcome.

You've weathered storms and basked in sunshine, each experience shaping you into who you are today. Trust in your abilities and your capacity to learn and adapt. Your opinions matter. Your feelings are valid. Your dreams are important. Nurture your self-esteem like a precious plant, giving it the care and attention it needs to flourish. As your confidence grows, so does your ability to shine your light into the world.

DEAR UNIVERSE,
I am confident in my abilities and value. My self-esteem grows stronger each day, empowering me to shine brightly.

*so be it,
so it is.*

self-care

YOU CAN'T POUR FROM AN EMPTY CUP. Prioritizing self-care isn't selfish; it's essential. Listen to your body and mind—they're always communicating with you. When you're tired, take time to rest. When you're stressed, take a little break. Nourish yourself with wholesome food, refreshing water, and activities that bring you joy. Set boundaries to protect your energy and peace. Make time for the things that make your soul sing, whether it's reading a book (like this one), taking a walk in nature, or creating some magnificent art.

DEAR UNIVERSE, may I prioritize my well-being, nurturing my mind, body, and soul. Self-care is my path to balance and fulfillment.

so be it,
so it is.

Remember, self-care looks different for everyone. Discover what truly rejuvenates you and make it a non-negotiable part of your routine. By taking care of yourself, you're better equipped to care for others and pursue your passions. You deserve to feel good in your body and calm in your mind. Embrace self-care as an act of self-respect and watch as it transforms your life.

6

DAY

self-respect

YOU ARE THE AUTHOR OF YOUR OWN STORY, the architect of your life. Every decision you make, every boundary you set, is a testament to your self-respect. Stand firm in your values, even when it's uncomfortable. Your time, your energy, your body—they are precious. Treat them as such. Don't compromise your integrity for fleeting approval or temporary gain. Remember, how you allow others to treat you sets the standard for your relationships. Speak to yourself with kindness and assertiveness. My history with negative self-talk has been quite challenging over the years. My inner "mean girl" often appears in fitting rooms trying on dresses or when I'm feeling a wave of PMS storm into my world. The only thing to do is acknowledge the temporary nature of the fleeting thoughts.

DEAR UNIVERSE, I honor myself with unwavering self-respect and dignity. My choices reflect my worth, and I stand tall in my truth.

so be it, so it is.

As you begin to manifest the magic of self-respect, you'll find that it radiates outward, influencing how the world interacts with you. Your self-respect is the foundation upon which you build a life of dignity and fulfillment.

SELF-LOVE AND ACCEPTANCE   137

7

self-discovery

EMBARK ON THE GREATEST ADVENTURE OF YOUR LIFE—the journey to your authentic self. You are a vast, unexplored Universe, filled with hidden talents, untapped potential, and surprising passions. Each day offers a new opportunity to peel back another layer, to uncover another facet of who you truly are. Be curious about your thoughts, your reactions, your desires. Question your beliefs and challenge your assumptions.

Try new experiences that push you out of your comfort zone—this is where the magic happens. What lights you up? What makes you feel alive? What values resonate deep in your core? As you discover these truths about yourself, embrace them fully. Let go of who you think you should be and step into who you actually are.

DEAR UNIVERSE,
I embrace the journey of self-discovery with open arms and a curious heart. Each day reveals new wonders within me.

so be it,
so it is.

self-reliance

YOU POSSESS AN INNER WELLSPRING OF STRENGTH, wisdom, and capability. Tap into it. Trust your instincts and your ability to navigate life's challenges. While it's valuable to seek advice, help, and support (especially when you really need it), remember that you are the expert on your own life. You have overcome obstacles before, and you will do so again. Cultivate skills that increase your independence. Learn to solve problems creatively.

Develop resilience by facing small challenges head-on. When you stumble, pick yourself up. When you're unsure, take a moment to center yourself and listen to your inner voice. It's okay to ask for help, but know that you have the power to find solutions within yourself. As you build self-reliance, you'll find a deep sense of confidence and freedom.

DEAR UNIVERSE,
I trust in my abilities and inner wisdom. I am capable and resilient, and I embody the energy of self-reliance in all aspects of my life.

so be it,
so it is.

9

inner strength

AIRPORT GOODBYES CAN REQUIRE SO MUCH inner strength. With older parents, I never know if it will be the last time I see them when they come to visit me from Australia. Those final moments before saying goodbye at the departure gate mean I have to take several deep breaths, as my heart races and I have to summon all of my strength to say my farewells.

In times like these, visualize a mighty river flowing through you, powerful and unstoppable. This is your inner strength—a force that has carried you through every trial and tribulation. It's the quiet determination that gets you out of bed on tough mornings, the resilience that helps you bounce back from setbacks.

Your inner strength is not about being invincible; it's about continuing even when you feel vulnerable. It's the courage to face your fears, to stand up for what's right, to be true to yourself in a world that often demands conformity. This strength grows with every challenge you overcome, every fear you face. It's the fire in your belly that fuels your dreams and the steady heartbeat that keeps you going when those dreams seem distant. Tap into this wellspring of power within you. Let it guide you, support you, and propel you forward.

DEAR UNIVERSE, my inner strength flows endlessly, guiding me through all of life's challenges. I am resilient, courageous, and unstoppable.

so be it, so it is.

inner harmony

IMAGINE A SYMPHONY PLAYING WITHIN YOU, each instrument representing a different aspect of your being—your thoughts, emotions, desires, and actions. When these elements work in harmony, you experience a profound sense of peace and alignment. Tune in to this inner harmony by listening to all parts of yourself with compassion and curiosity. Acknowledge your conflicting desires without judgment. Seek balance between work and rest, solitude, creativity, connection, giving, and receiving.

Practice mindfulness to stay present and grounded. When you feel out of sync, take a deep breath and gently guide yourself back to center. Remember, harmony doesn't mean the absence of discord; it's the ability to find balance amid life's ever-changing rhythms. As you nurture inner harmony, you'll move through the world with greater ease and grace, better equipped to handle whatever comes your way.

DEAR UNIVERSE,
I manifest inner harmony, balancing all aspects of my being. Peace and alignment flow through me effortlessly.

so be it,
so it is.

11

self-assurance

YOU ARE A FORCE TO BE RECKONED WITH, a beacon of confidence in a world of uncertainty. Self-assurance isn't about knowing everything; it's about trusting your ability to handle whatever comes your way. Stand tall in your convictions, speak your mind with clarity, and pursue your goals with unwavering determination. When doubt creeps in, remind yourself of past victories, no matter how small. Your experiences have shaped you into the capable individual you are today. Embrace challenges as opportunities to prove your mettle. Remember, self-assurance is like a muscle—the more you exercise it, the stronger it becomes. Take calculated risks, make decisions with conviction, and learn from the outcomes.

As you try on the essence of self-assurance, you'll find doors opening, relationships deepening, and opportunities multiplying. Your confidence is magnetic, inspiring those around you to believe in themselves too.

DEAR UNIVERSE,
I radiate self-assurance in all that I do. My confidence grows stronger each day, empowering me to embrace life fully.

so be it,
so it is.

self-expression

EXPRESS YOUR VOICE BOLDLY, authentically, unapologetically. Whether through words, art, movement, or simply the way you live your life, your self-expression is a gift to the world. Don't dim your light to make others comfortable. Embrace your quirks, your passions, your unconventional ideas. They are the brushstrokes that make the masterpiece of you. Experiment with different forms of expression until you find what resonates. Maybe it's writing, painting, dancing, or problem-solving. Whatever it is, do it with your whole heart. Let your truth flow through you, raw and unfiltered.

Your self-expression has the power to inspire, heal, and connect. It's the bridge between your inner world and the outer reality. As you express yourself fully, you'll discover new depths within and forge genuine connections without.

DEAR UNIVERSE,
I present myself freely and authentically with the energy of self-expression, sharing my unique gifts with the world. My voice rings true and clear.

so be it,
so it is.

13

self-fulfillment

IMAGINE STANDING AT THE PEAK OF A MOUNTAIN, surveying the path you've climbed. That sense of accomplishment, of being exactly where you're meant to be—that's self-fulfillment. It's not about reaching a final destination, but about aligning your actions with your values and purpose. Pursue what lights you up from within, not what others expect of you. Set meaningful goals that challenge and excite you.

DEAR UNIVERSE,
I live in alignment with my true purpose, finding deep self-fulfillment in my journey. My life is rich with meaning and joy.

so be it,
so it is.

Celebrate your progress, no matter how small. Find joy in the journey, not just the outcome. Remember, self-fulfillment is deeply personal. What fills your cup may be different from others, and that's okay. Listen to your inner voice, trust your instincts, and have the courage to forge your own path. As you live in alignment with your true self, you'll experience a deep sense of satisfaction and purpose that radiates through every aspect of your life.

self-understanding

YOU ARE A COMPLEX TAPESTRY OF EXPERIENCES, emotions, and aspirations. Take the time to explore the intricate patterns that make you who you are. Self-understanding is the key that unlocks your potential and paves the way for authentic living. Reflect on your reactions, examine your beliefs, and question your habits. Where do they come from? Do they still serve you? Be honest with yourself about your strengths and areas for growth. Embrace your contradictions—they make you beautifully human. Practice self-awareness in your daily life. Notice your thoughts, feelings, and behaviors without judgment.

DEAR UNIVERSE,
I embrace deep self-understanding, uncovering new truths about myself each day. My self-awareness guides me toward authentic living.

so be it,
so it is.

As you deepen your self-understanding, you'll make choices that align with your true self, communicate more effectively, and navigate relationships with greater ease. Remember, self-understanding is an ongoing journey. Be patient and compassionate with yourself as you uncover new layers of your being.

15

self-validation

YOUR WORTH DOESN'T NEED EXTERNAL CONFIRMATION. You are enough, just as you are, in this very moment. Practice validating your own feelings, decisions, and experiences. When you accomplish something, acknowledge it. When you're hurting, honor that pain. Your emotions are valid, your efforts are significant, your dreams are worthy. Stop seeking approval from others and start approving of yourself. Trust your judgment, even when it goes against the grain. Celebrate your uniqueness instead of trying to fit into someone else's mold.

Remember, no one else can define your value or dictate your path. You are the author of your story, the judge of your worth. As you give yourself self-validation, you'll find a deep well of inner peace and confidence that can't be shaken by external opinions or circumstances.

DEAR UNIVERSE,
I validate my own worth, honoring my feelings and experiences. My self-validation is unwavering and complete.

so be it,
so it is.

unconditional love

IMAGINE A LOVE SO VAST, it encompasses every part of you—your triumphs and failures, your light and shadow. This is unconditional love, and it starts with you. Embrace yourself fully, without judgment or conditions. Love yourself on your best days and your worst. When you make mistakes, respond with compassion instead of criticism. Celebrate your uniqueness, quirks and all. This self-love isn't selfish; it's the foundation for all other relationships. As you nurture unconditional love for yourself, you'll find it easier to extend that same love to others.

You'll become a beacon of acceptance and understanding in a world that often judges too harshly. Remember, you are worthy of love simply because you exist. No achievements or perfection required. Let this unconditional love fill you up, overflow, and touch everything you do.

DEAR UNIVERSE,
I embrace unconditional love for myself and others. My heart overflows with acceptance, compassion, and understanding for all beings.

so be it,
so it is.

17

personal growth

YOU ARE A GARDEN IN CONSTANT BLOOM. Each challenge you face, each lesson you learn, is another seed planted in the fertile soil of your being. Embrace the process of growth, even when it's uncomfortable. Push beyond your comfort zone, for that's where true expansion happens. Seek out new experiences, perspectives, and knowledge. Let curiosity be your guide. Remember, growth isn't always linear—sometimes you'll take two steps forward and one step back. That's okay. Each setback is an opportunity for a comeback.

Celebrate your progress, no matter how small. Reflect on how far you've come and let it inspire you to keep reaching higher. As you stand in the energy of personal growth, you'll discover strengths you never knew you had and possibilities you never imagined.

DEAR UNIVERSE,
I embrace continuous personal growth, blossoming into my highest potential. Every experience nurtures my evolution and expansion.

so be it,
so it is.

inner peace

WITHIN YOU LIES A SANCTUARY OF CALM, a still point in the chaos of life. It's always there, waiting for you to turn inward and find it. Breathe deeply and feel the tension melt away. Let go of what you can't control and focus on the present moment. Inner peace isn't about eliminating all problems; it's about finding tranquility amid the storms. Practice mindfulness in your daily life. Notice the simple joys—the warmth of sunlight, the taste of your favorite food, the sound of laughter.

When worries arise, acknowledge them without getting caught up in their story. Remember, you are not your thoughts. You are the peaceful observer of those thoughts. As you align with the energy of inner peace, you'll move through life with greater ease and resilience.

DEAR UNIVERSE,
I cultivate unshakeable inner peace, remaining calm and centered in all situations. Tranquility flows through me effortlessly.

so be it,
so it is.

19

self-empowerment

YOU HOLD THE KEY TO YOUR OWN POWER. It's not something given to you by others, but a force that resides within. Recognize the strength in your choices, your voice, your actions. Take responsibility for your life and the energy you bring to each situation. Set clear intentions and follow through with purposeful action. When faced with obstacles, remind yourself of past victories. You've overcome challenges before, and you will again. Trust in your ability to shape your reality. Speak your truth, even when your voice shakes.

DEAR UNIVERSE,
I claim self-empowerment, shaping my life with intention and courage. I am the architect of my destiny.

*so be it,
so it is.*

Stand firm in your convictions while remaining open to growth. As you embrace self-empowerment, you'll find yourself stepping into leadership roles, inspiring others, and creating positive change in your world.

authenticity

YOU ARE A ONE-OF-A-KIND MASTERPIECE. There's no one else in the world quite like you, with your unique blend of experiences, perspectives, and gifts. Embrace your true self, quirks and all. Let go of the masks you wear to fit in or please others. Speak your truth, even if your voice shakes. Live according to your values, not society's expectations. Authenticity isn't always easy, but it's infinitely rewarding. As you align your outer life with your inner truth, you'll attract genuine connections and opportunities that resonate with your soul.

Remember, the world doesn't need another copy. It needs you—the real, unfiltered, magnificent you.

DEAR UNIVERSE,
I embrace the energy of authenticity fully, shining my unique light without fear or hesitation. My truth resonates powerfully in the world.

so be it,
so it is.

21

self-belief

PICTURE A BEAUTIFUL BLOOMING BLOSSOM TREE, its roots deep in the earth, its branches reaching for the sky. That tree is you—grounded in your values, yet always growing toward your dreams and blooming with possibility. Believe in your capacity to weather any storm, to bend without breaking. Trust in your ability to learn, adapt, and overcome. When doubt creeps in, remind yourself of past successes. You've faced challenges before and emerged stronger. Your potential is limitless. Believe in your ideas, your skills, your heart. Even when others don't see your vision, hold fast to your dreams.

DEAR UNIVERSE,
I believe in myself wholeheartedly, trusting in my abilities and potential. My self-belief grows stronger each day.

so be it,
so it is.

As you embody self-belief, you'll find the courage to take risks, to speak up, to pursue your passions with unwavering determination.

self-contentment

CONTENTMENT IS NOT ABOUT having everything you want, but wanting everything you have. Embrace the present moment, finding joy in the simple things. Appreciate your journey, with all its twists and turns. Recognize that you are enough, just as you are. This doesn't mean giving up on growth or ambition; it means finding peace with where you are while working toward where you want to be. Practice gratitude daily. Notice the abundance already present in your life. Let go of comparisons and embrace your unique path. As you build self-contentment within yourself, you'll find a deep well of inner peace that sustains you through life's ups and downs.

DEAR UNIVERSE,
I embody the energy of self-contentment with who I am and where I am in life. Gratitude and peace flow through me abundantly.

so be it,
so it is.

23

inner joy

HAVE YOU EVER FELT SO OVERWHELMED by joy that you felt like you'd burst? Perhaps you just received some excellent news or manifested a miracle. This feeling should be bottled. It's truly magnificent.

Joy is not just a fleeting emotion, but a radiant light that shines from within. It's always there, even when obscured by life's challenges. Reconnect with your inner child, the part of you that finds wonder in the ordinary. Laugh often, play freely, love deeply. Seek out experiences that light you up from the inside. Contribute to relationships that nourish your soul. Find purpose in serving others. Remember, joy is not dependent on external circumstances.

It's a choice you make, moment by moment. As you tap into your inner joy, you'll become a beacon of light, uplifting those around you and transforming your world.

DEAR UNIVERSE,
I radiate inner joy from the depths of my being, finding delight in each moment. My inner light shines brightly, uplifting all.

so be it,
so it is.

self-reflection

IMAGINE YOUR MIND AS A STILL LAKE, reflecting the sky above. Self-reflection is the practice of looking into those waters, seeing yourself clearly and honestly. Take time each day to pause and turn inward. Examine your thoughts, feelings, and actions without judgment. What motivates you? What holds you back? What lessons can you learn from your experiences? Self-reflection isn't about criticism, but about understanding and growth. It's the compass that guides you toward your true north. As you dive into this practice, you'll gain invaluable insights, make more intentional choices, and live with greater authenticity and purpose.

DEAR UNIVERSE,
I embrace regular self-reflection, gaining deep insights into my true self. Clarity and wisdom guide my journey of growth.

so be it,
so it is.

25

personal acceptance

YOU ARE A BEAUTIFUL MOSAIC OF strengths and weaknesses, triumphs and struggles. Accept all parts of yourself—the light and the shadow, the polished and the rough. This acceptance isn't resignation; it's the foundation for genuine growth and change. Acknowledge your imperfections without judgment. Celebrate your uniqueness.

Let go of who you think you should be and embrace who you truly are. As you practice personal acceptance, you'll find a deep sense of peace and authenticity. You'll be free to grow and evolve, not from a place of self-rejection, but from a place of self-love.

DEAR UNIVERSE,
I practice personal acceptance, embracing all aspects of who I am. My self-love grows deeper and more complete each day.

so be it,
so it is.

self-confidence

STAND TALL IN YOUR OWN POWER. You are capable of amazing things. Trust in your abilities, your judgment, your worth. Self-confidence isn't about being perfect; it's about knowing you can handle whatever comes your way. Speak your mind with clarity and conviction. Take up space unapologetically. When self-doubt creeps in, remind yourself of past successes. You've overcome challenges before, and you will again. As you begin to build self-confidence, you'll find doors opening, opportunities multiplying, and your influence growing. Your confidence is magnetic, inspiring others to believe in themselves too.

DEAR UNIVERSE,
I radiate unshakeable self-confidence in all areas of my life. My belief in myself grows stronger each day.

so be it,
so it is.

27

emotional healing

VISUALIZE YOUR HEART AS A GARDEN. Some parts are in full bloom, while others need tending. Emotional healing is the process of nurturing those wounded areas back to health. Acknowledge your pain without judgment. Feel your feelings fully, knowing they are valid and temporary. Practice self-compassion as you navigate difficult emotions. Seek support when needed, whether from loved ones or professionals. Remember, healing isn't linear. Some days will be easier than others, and that's okay. As you commit to this journey of emotional healing, you'll find greater resilience, deeper connections, and a renewed sense of inner peace.

DEAR UNIVERSE,
I embrace emotional healing, tending to my heart with compassion and care. My inner wounds transform into sources of strength and wisdom.

so be it,
so it is.

inner serenity

IMAGINE A LUSH MEADOW IN SPRINGTIME, where the air is crisp and every blade of grass sparkles with morning dew, catching the first rays of sunlight. The meadow, like your inner state, is vibrant and alive, yet still and serene, holding the promise of growth and new beginnings. This tranquil scene exists within you, a wellspring of inner serenity always accessible. Amid life's chaos, remember to turn inward and tap into this peaceful core. Breathe deeply, letting tension melt away. Practice mindfulness, anchoring yourself in the present moment. Let go of what you can't control, focusing instead on your response to life's challenges. Cultivate patience, both with yourself and others. As you nurture your inner serenity, you'll move through life with greater ease and grace, remaining calm and centered even in turbulent times.

DEAR UNIVERSE,
I cultivate deep inner serenity, remaining peaceful amid life's storms. Tranquility flows through me in every moment.

*so be it,
so it is.*

29

self-awareness

YOU ARE A VAST UNIVERSE OF THOUGHTS, emotions, and experiences. Self-awareness is the telescope that allows you to explore this inner cosmos. Pay attention to your reactions, your habits, your patterns. Notice without judgment. Ask yourself why you think, feel, and act the way you do. Be curious about your motivations and fears. This self-knowledge is power—it allows you to make conscious choices rather than operating on autopilot. As you deepen your self-awareness, you'll communicate more effectively, navigate relationships with greater ease, and align your actions with your true values.

DEAR UNIVERSE,
I cultivate deep self-awareness, understanding my inner world with clarity and compassion. My self-knowledge guides me toward authentic living.

so be it,
so it is.

DAY

30

inner balance

WHEN I LIVED IN GOTHENBURG, SWEDEN, it was around 1 a.m. one morning when I decided to walk home after drinking two cocktails. The only catch was that it had snowed heavily and I was wearing high heels. This is not usually a good combination at the best of times. I had to summon all of my inner balance to make it home without falling on my caboose. Visualizing staying upright was my best kept secret.

Picture yourself as a tightrope walker, gracefully moving forward while maintaining perfect equilibrium. This is inner balance—the art of harmonizing different aspects of your life and self. Nurture your body, mind, and spirit equally. Find the sweet spot between work and rest, giving and receiving, solitude and connection. When life tilts you one way, gently adjust to regain your center. Remember, balance isn't about perfection; it's about flexibility and adaptability. As you find your inner balance, you'll move through life with greater ease and resilience, able to weather any storm while maintaining your inner harmony.

DEAR UNIVERSE, I maintain perfect inner balance, harmonizing all aspects of my being. Equilibrium and peace flow through me effortlessly.

so be it, so it is.

31

self-appreciation

GIVE YOURSELF A PAT ON THE BACK. You are a masterpiece in progress, a unique blend of strengths, experiences, and potential. Take time each day to appreciate your journey—the obstacles you've overcome, the growth you've achieved, the dreams you're pursuing. Celebrate your quirks and idiosyncrasies; they make you uniquely you. Acknowledge your efforts, not just your achievements. Be as kind to yourself as you would be to a dear friend.

As you lean into the magic of self-appreciation, you'll build a strong foundation of self-worth that can't be shaken by external circumstances. Your inner light will shine brighter, inspiring others to appreciate themselves too.

DEAR UNIVERSE,
I deeply embody self-appreciation, celebrating my unique journey and essence. My self-love grows stronger each day.

so be it,
so it is.

MONTH 6

positivity and optimism

A positive mindset can transform your approach to life. This month, we emphasize the power of positivity and the importance of cultivating an optimistic outlook. It's time to see the glass as half full, instead of half empty.

Put on your rose-colored glasses and remember that embracing optimism fosters resilience and motivation, helping you navigate challenges with a constructive attitude. By focusing on the positive, you attract more opportunities and success.

REMEMBER: Positivity is a powerful force. Keep your outlook bright, stay resilient, and observe how your life flourishes with renewed energy and beautiful purpose.

hopeful

HAVE YOU EVER NOTICED HOW HOPE can light up even the darkest corners of your life? You are stronger than you know, and brighter days are always on the horizon. Every challenge you face is an opportunity for growth, and every setback is an invitation from the Universe to rise above your limitations and thrive. The manifestation of hopefulness always appears when you can muster the courage to keep going.

Remember, the sun always rises after the night, just as hope always emerges after hardship. Your resilience is your superpower, and it will guide you through any storm. Embrace the power of hope, for it is the fuel that drives dreams into reality.

DEAR UNIVERSE,
I am hopeful, knowing that every challenge leads to growth and every setback paves the way for success.

so be it,
so it is.

joyfulness

JOYFULNESS IS NOT JUST A FLEETING EMOTION; it's a choice you make every day, sometimes in every moment. You have the power to find happiness in the smallest times of presence—a warm cup of coffee, a kind smile from a stranger, or the gentle rustle of leaves in the wind. Embrace these little pockets of joy, and watch how they transform your entire day. Your ability to find delight in the ordinary is extraordinary.

Let your laughter ring out, your smile shine bright, and your heart overflow with the pure, unbridled joy of being alive. My mum always told me when I was little that life is not a dress rehearsal and to find joy and embody it.

DEAR UNIVERSE,
I choose joyfulness in every moment, finding delight in life's simple pleasures and radiating happiness to all around me.

*so be it,
so it is.*

optimistic

IT'S TIME TO PUT ON YOUR ROSE-COLORED GLASSES. The world is full of possibilities, and you hold the key to unlocking them. Your optimistic outlook is the lens through which you view life, turning obstacles into opportunities and challenges into chances for growth.

Every day is a fresh start, a blank canvas waiting for you to paint your dreams upon it. Embrace the power of positive thinking, for it has the ability to transform not just your mind, but your entire reality. Your optimism is contagious, inspiring those around you to see the brighter side of life.

DEAR UNIVERSE,
I embrace an optimistic outlook, seeing endless possibilities in every situation and inspiring positivity in those around me.

*so be it,
so it is.*

positive

YOU CAN BE A BEACON OF positivity in a world that sometimes forgets to look on the bright side. Your attitude is not just a reflection of the world you see, but a powerful force that shapes it.

Every positive thought you nurture is a seed planted in the garden of your life, destined to bloom into beautiful realities. Your ability to find the silver lining, even in the stormiest clouds, is your greatest strength. Remember, a positive mind attracts positive experiences, so keep shining your light.

DEAR UNIVERSE,
I radiate positivity, attracting abundance and joy into my life and spreading light to everyone I encounter.

so be it,
so it is.

5

bright

HOW BRIGHTLY DO YOU SHINE WHEN you let your true self emerge? Have you ever stopped to see the true and beautiful brightness of you? If you haven't, then now is the time.

You are a brilliant star in the vast Universe, uniquely positioned to illuminate the world with your gifts. Your brightness isn't just about being happy all the time; it's about bringing light to others, even when you're navigating your own shadows. Every time you share your knowledge, your kindness, or your smile, you're brightening someone's day. Never dim your light to fit in—the world needs your brilliance. Shine and lead by example.

DEAR UNIVERSE,
I embrace shining my unique bright light to illuminate the path for myself and others.

so be it,
so it is.

cheerful

CHEERFULNESS IS YOUR SECRET WEAPON AGAINST life's challenges. We all know the person that likes to poop on someone else's parade . . . but when this happens to you . . . don't let it. Rise above it and choose the cheerful path.

Cheerfulness is the gentle smile that creeps onto your face even on tough days, the quiet chuckle at a silly joke, the spring in your step as you tackle your to-do list. Your cheerful spirit is a gift not just to yourself, but to everyone around you. It's contagious, spreading joy and lightness wherever you go. Cultivate this cheerfulness, nurture it, and watch how it transforms not only your day but the days of those around you.

DEAR UNIVERSE,
I cultivate a cheerful spirit, spreading joy and lightness to everyone I encounter, transforming each day into a celebration.

so be it,
so it is.

7

spirited

YOUR SPIRIT IS AN UNSTOPPABLE FORCE, a wellspring of energy and enthusiasm that propels you forward. It's the fire in your belly that drives you to chase your dreams, the passion that fuels your pursuits. Think of the issues and causes that you would gladly get a little heated over. This is the beautiful essence of you getting spirited. I can tell you, if someone says anything bad or negative about my friends or family, I can get quite spirited. It's a loyalty thing where you are called from the depths of your spirit and character to protect the energy of your loved ones.

DEAR UNIVERSE,
my spirited nature ignites passion in everything I do, inspiring others and transforming challenges into exciting adventures.

*so be it,
so it is.*

This spirited nature of yours is a gift—it's what makes you stand out in a crowd, what makes people gravitate toward your energy. Embrace your zest for life, let your enthusiasm shine through in everything you do. Your spirited approach to life is not just inspiring; it's transformative.

encouraging

YOU'VE GOT THIS. WHATEVER TODAY BRINGS FOR YOU, please know that you have everything you need to succeed. You also have the power to lift others up with your words and actions. Your encouragement is like water to a seed, nurturing growth and potential in those around you. Every time you offer a kind word, a supportive gesture, or a listening ear, you're creating a ripple effect of positivity.

Don't underestimate the impact of your encouragement—it could be the very thing that gives someone the courage to chase their dreams. Be generous with your support, for in lifting others, you also elevate yourself.

DEAR UNIVERSE,
I am a source of unwavering and encouraging energy that nurtures growth and potential in others while elevating my own spirit.

so be it,
so it is.

confident

DO YOU REALIZE THE INCREDIBLE POWER that lies within you? Confidence is not about being perfect; it's about trusting yourself and your abilities. It's the quiet assurance that you can handle whatever life throws your way. Your confidence is like a beacon, guiding you through uncertain waters and inspiring others to believe in themselves too.

Embrace your strengths, acknowledge your worth, and stand tall in your uniqueness. The world responds to the energy you put out—so radiate confidence and watch doors open.

I never thought in a million years that I would speak on stages around the world. I was always very shy and timid as a child. However, to share my mission and message with the world required confidence to not make it about myself so that I could help others.

DEAR UNIVERSE,
I radiate unshakeable confident energy, trusting in my abilities and inspiring others to embrace their own power and potential.

*so be it,
so it is.*

DAY

10

uplifted

FEELING UPLIFTED IS LIKE RIDING ON a magical pink fluffy cloud of positivity, seeing the world from a higher perspective. You have the power to elevate not just your own spirits, but those of everyone around you.

Every time you choose to focus on the good, to see the potential for growth in challenges, you're lifting yourself higher. This uplifted state is contagious—your positive energy has the power to raise the vibration of an entire room. Embrace this feeling, nurture it, and watch how it transforms your life and the lives of those around you.

DEAR UNIVERSE,
I am consistently uplifted, seeing the world from a higher perspective and elevating the spirits of those around me.

so be it,
so it is.

happy

WHEN WAS THE LAST TIME YOU WERE TRULY HAPPY? I'm hoping it's now as you are reading this book! This is a big question, but it's an important one to ask yourself. Happiness is not a destination, but a way of traveling through life. It's found in the little moments—a child's laughter, a beautiful sunset, a task well done, eating a bag of chips that soothes an intense craving for salt.

You have the power to create your own happiness, to find joy in the everyday miracles that surround you. Your smile is a gift to the world, you know this one, where your eyes light up. Your laughter is a melody that brightens the day and soothes the souls of others around you. Embrace this happiness, let it fill you up and overflow to others. Remember, a happy heart is a magnet for miracles.

DEAR UNIVERSE,
I create and radiate happy energy in every moment, finding joy in life's simple pleasures and spreading smiles wherever I go.

so be it,
so it is.

content

IN THE FAIRYTALE, Goldilocks tried all of the porridge until she found the one that was "just right."

Contentment is the art of finding peace in the present moment sometimes after experiencing the contrast of many different things. However, you don't need to wait for everything to be perfect to be content—you can choose contentment right now. It's in the deep breath you take, the warmth of the sun on your face, the comfort of your own company, crawling into bed after a long day and snuggling up with a cozy blanket. For me personally, contentment is finishing a really good writing session, taking a sip of hot tea with a piece of chocolate, and long and loving hugs with my babies.

This sense of contentment is your anchor in the storm of life, keeping you grounded and peaceful no matter what's happening around you. Embrace this contentment, for it is the key to true happiness.

DEAR UNIVERSE, I embrace the essence of being content in every moment, finding peace and joy in the present, regardless of external circumstances.

so be it,
so it is.

13

appreciative

WHAT IF YOU LOOKED AT YOUR life through a lens of appreciation? Every challenge becomes a teacher, every setback a well-placed stepping stone. Your ability to appreciate not just the good times, but the lessons in the hard times, is a superpower. It transforms your entire experience of life. When you cultivate appreciation, you train your mind to see the beauty in everything. This grateful perspective not only enhances your own joy but also inspires those around you to find reasons to be thankful.

DEAR UNIVERSE,
I cultivate deep awareness for being appreciative for all aspects of life, finding beauty in every moment and inspiring gratitude in others.

so be it,
so it is.

I remember when I would find furniture on the side of the road when I was setting up my first apartment as a single mother. I would see the potential to clean it up and make the chair or table useful. I was so appreciative for whatever I would find that could help me out in my situation. The more appreciation I felt, the more stuff would show up to appreciate.

lively

LIFE PULSES THROUGH YOU WITH AN electric energy. Can you feel it? I hope you can. Your liveliness is a force of nature, drawing people in and inspiring them to embrace their own vitality. It's in the spring in your step, the enthusiasm in your voice, the sparkle in your eye.

This zest for life is contagious, breathing energy into every room you enter. Embrace your lively spirit, let it fuel your pursuits and light up your world. Remember, your energy is your signature—make it a vibrant one. Imagine yourself celebrating your hundredth birthday (unless you are already over one hundred) and feeling how lively and vibrant you feel. Never let your age define how vibrant you believe you should feel.

DEAR UNIVERSE, my lively spirit energizes every aspect of my life, inspiring vitality and joy in myself and those around me.

so be it, so it is.

15

enthusiastic

IN WRITING, ENTHUSIASM IS SHOWN IN exclamation points! Or perhaps ALL CAPS. We all know that one person in our lives that is a little too enthusiastic when it comes to communication, but it's an important aspect to embody. Enthusiasm is the fire that fuels your dreams. It's the excited flutter in your chest when you embark on a new project, the surge of energy when you're passionate about something.

DEAR UNIVERSE, my enthusiastic nature ignites passion in everything I do, turning ordinary moments into extraordinary adventures and inspiring others along the way.

so be it, so it is.

Your enthusiasm is a magnet, drawing opportunities and like-minded people toward you. It turns ordinary tasks into adventures and challenges into exciting quests. Embrace this enthusiasm, let it color your world and inspire others. Remember, an enthusiastic mind is a powerful mind.

heartwarming

YOU HAVE THE POWER TO WARM hearts with your presence. You have such a big heart. Your kindness, your smile, your genuine care for others—these are the embers that keep the world's heart glowing. Every act of compassion, every word of encouragement you utter, every gesture of love you offer is like a warm hug to someone's soul. This ability to touch hearts is a precious gift.

Embrace it, nurture it, and watch how it transforms not just individual lives, but the very atmosphere around you.

DEAR UNIVERSE,
I radiate heartwarming compassion, touching hearts and transforming lives with every kind gesture and loving word.

*so be it,
so it is.*

17

grateful

HAVE YOU PAUSED TODAY TO COUNT YOUR BLESSINGS? Gratitude is the magic that turns what you have into enough. Your ability to appreciate the small things—a warm bed, a loving friend, an unexpected gift—is a superpower. It shifts your focus from what's lacking to the abundance that surrounds you in each and every moment.

This grateful heart of yours is a magnet for more goodness. Embrace this gratitude, let it fill your days with joy and your nights with peace. Remember, a grateful heart is a magnet for miracles.

DEAR UNIVERSE,
I am deeply grateful for all the blessings in my life, attracting more abundance and joy with every thankful thought.

*so be it,
so it is.*

invigorated

I SPENT MONTHS WORKING TIRELESSLY TO launch a program that ultimately failed. Despite our hopes for a big, successful launch, we saw hardly any sales. Overwhelmed with anxiety, I knew I needed to ground myself. I decided to take a cold plunge in the bay at Sag Harbor in winter. The freezing temperature made the water feel like tiny pins piercing my skin as I cautiously immersed myself into the clear, blue bay. It changed my state immediately—I felt invigorated. I highly recommend that you try this for yourself (unless you are told otherwise by a medical professional).

Feel the energy coursing through your veins, the vitality that makes you feel alive and ready to take on the world. This invigorated state is your natural birthright—it's the zest for life that propels you forward, that makes you jump out of bed excited for what the day will bring. Your invigorated spirit is contagious, inspiring others to shake off lethargy and embrace life fully.

Nurture this energy, feed it with positive thoughts and healthy habits, and watch how it transforms your life, and your mood if you need it to.

DEAR UNIVERSE,
I am constantly invigorated, filled with boundless energy and enthusiasm that inspires vitality in myself and others.

so be it,
so it is.

energetic

EVERYTHING IS ENERGY AND YOU ARE NO DIFFERENT. We live in a society that likes to pretend that the energetics and vibration of what unfolds in our lives are not important. We're taught to only focus on what we can see and quantify, not necessarily tuning in to the awareness of the unseen world.

DEAR UNIVERSE, my abundant soul fuels my passions in an energetic way. It ignites my dreams, and inspires those around me to embrace their own vibrant potential.

so be it, so it is.

In fact, your energy is a force to be reckoned with. It's the spring in your step, the enthusiasm in your voice, the tiny twinkle in your eye. This vibrant energy of yours is not just a personal asset—it's a gift to the world. It has the power to uplift, inspire, and motivate those around you. Embrace this energy, channel it into your passions and goals. Let it fuel your dreams and light up your path. Remember, your energy is contagious—make it a positive epidemic.

refreshing

I LIVED IN LAS VEGAS FOR ABOUT SIX YEARS, where the summer heat was scorching. Grocery shopping in temperatures exceeding 100 degrees made the walk from the parking lot to the store feel almost unbearable. The moment the sliding doors of Whole Foods opened and the cool blast of air conditioning hit me, it felt incredibly refreshing. A refreshing experience like that is a reset.

Like a cool breeze on a hot day, your presence brings refreshment to those around you. Your unique perspective, your authentic self, your ability to see things differently— these are the qualities that make you a breath of fresh air in a world that often feels stagnant. Embrace this refreshing nature of yours. Let your originality shine, your creativity flow, your unique voice be heard. You have the power to rejuvenate not just yourself, but everyone you encounter.

DEAR UNIVERSE,
I am a refreshing presence in the world, bringing new perspectives and rejuvenating energy to every situation and interaction.

so be it,
so it is.

renewed

EVERY MORNING OFFERS A CHANCE FOR RENEWAL. Make that day today. You wake up with a clean slate, a fresh opportunity to rewrite your story no matter what level of upheaval you have experienced in your past. This sense of renewal is not just about new beginnings; it's about the continuous process of growth and transformation. Embrace this renewal in every aspect of your life—in your thoughts, your relationships, your goals.

Let go of what no longer serves you and make space for new experiences and insights. Remember, you are constantly evolving, always becoming a newer, better version of yourself. The reason your soul came here to earth is to learn and to keep manifesting positive and powerful change for yourself.

DEAR UNIVERSE,
I embrace the energy of feeling renewed in every moment, constantly evolving and growing into the best version of myself.

so be it,
so it is.

satisfied

SATISFACTION COMES FROM WITHIN. It's not about having everything, but appreciating what you have. Whether it's in life or in the bedroom, being able to express your needs and desires is crucial. Your ability to find contentment in the present moment and to savor life's simple pleasures is a precious gift.

This sense of satisfaction doesn't mean you stop growing or dreaming; rather, it provides a solid foundation from which you can reach for the stars. Embrace this satisfaction, let it fill you with peace and gratitude. Remember, a satisfied soul is a magnet for abundance. So speak up, whether it's about your goals or your needs in intimate moments—true satisfaction is about feeling heard and fulfilled.

DEAR UNIVERSE,
I am deeply satisfied with my life, appreciating all that I have while still dreaming and striving for growth.

so be it,
so it is.

23

gleeful

JOY BUBBLES UP WITHIN YOU LIKE sparkling champagne. Your ability to find delight in the smallest things and approach life with a sense of playfulness and wonder is a precious gift. This gleeful spirit of yours is like the boundless energy of a child, brimming with curiosity and unbridled enthusiasm. It's contagious, lighting up rooms and lifting spirits wherever you go.

Embrace this glee, let it infuse your days with laughter and lightheartedness. Dance in the rain, chase butterflies, and relish the simple joys that life offers. Your joyful heart is a beacon of light in this world, a reminder that life is too short to be serious all the time. By nurturing your inner child and celebrating the magic in everyday moments, you inspire others to do the same.

DEAR UNIVERSE, my heart feels gleeful, filling my life with laughter and spreading joy to everyone I encounter.

so be it,
so it is.

thankful

GRATITUDE, A KEY TOOL IN MANIFESTATION, unlocks life's fullness. Being thankful, even in tough times, is a superpower that shifts focus from lack to abundance. Each "thank-you" is like a prayer, acknowledging the good and inviting more. This is why we are diving into this one again.

Embrace thankfulness, letting it color your perception and guide your actions. Imagine gratitude as a beacon, attracting positivity and miracles. Start each day with gratitude, letting it touch every part of your life. In every interaction, find something to appreciate; in every challenge, discover a blessing.

A thankful heart transforms your life and lights the way for others. Remember, a grateful heart is a magnet for miracles. Let gratitude flow, and watch as the Universe responds, filling your life with endless wonders and joy.

DEAR UNIVERSE,
I am profoundly thankful for all the blessings in my life, recognizing abundance in every moment and attracting more goodness.

so be it,
so it is.

25

motivated

WHAT DRIVES YOU FORWARD? WHAT LIGHTS a little fire under your bum and makes you take action? Your motivation is the engine of your dreams, the force that propels you toward your goals. It's the fire in your belly that gets you out of bed each morning, ready to tackle the day. Sometimes you just need to decide that today is the day to take action.

This motivation isn't just about achieving; it's about growing, learning, and becoming the best version of yourself. Embrace this motivation, let it fuel your actions and inspire your decisions. Remember, a motivated mind is an unstoppable force.

DEAR UNIVERSE,
I am powerfully motivated, driven by passion and purpose to achieve my goals and inspire others along the way.

so be it,
so it is.

26

DAY

comforting

HAVE YOU EVER FELT COMPLETELY SAFE in someone's embrace? Has anyone ever reassured you when you were emotionally overwhelmed? The essence of providing and receiving comfort is invaluable.

Your presence is a soothing balm to those around you. The warmth of your smile, the gentleness in your voice, the compassion in your actions—these qualities make you a source of comfort in a sometimes harsh world. This ability to provide solace and support is a precious gift.

Embrace it, nurture it, and let it flow freely to those who need it. Remember, in comforting others, you also find comfort yourself. Also remember, it will all be okay.

DEAR UNIVERSE,
I am a comforting source of solace, offering warmth and support to those around me while finding peace within myself.

so be it,
so it is.

27

playful

I LIKE TO MESS WITH PEOPLE that I love and be playful with pranks, wild goose chases, and random surprises. Actually, I'll do almost anything if I know it will make my loved ones laugh. For instance, I'll jump out from behind a corner and scare my children. They'll scream and then laugh. We all will. It's hilarious!

DEAR UNIVERSE,
I embrace my playful spirit, approaching life with joy, creativity, and wonder, inspiring lightheartedness in myself and others.

so be it,
so it is.

Life is too important to be taken seriously all the time. Your playful spirit is a reminder to find joy in the journey, to approach challenges with creativity and humor. This playfulness of yours is not childishness, but a childlike wonder that sees the world as a playground of possibilities.

Embrace this playful nature, let it infuse your days with laughter and your work with creativity. Remember, a playful heart is an open heart, ready to receive life's gifts.

reassured

REASSURANCE IS ALWAYS THERE IF YOU NEED IT. Just ask the Universe.

Confidence blooms within you like a flower turning toward the sun. You are exactly where you need to be, learning the lessons you need to learn. This sense of reassurance isn't about knowing everything; it's about trusting in your ability to handle whatever comes your way and trusting that the Universe has your back. Your inner strength is a wellspring of comfort, reminding you that you've overcome challenges before and can do so again. Embrace this reassurance, let it calm your fears and steady your path. Remember, you are more capable than you know and, more often than not, than you think you are.

DEAR UNIVERSE,
I am deeply reassured, trusting in my journey and my ability to overcome any challenge that comes my way.

so be it,
so it is.

29

warmth

YOUR WARMTH IS LIKE A COZY, fluffy blanket on a chilly day, enveloping others in comfort and care. It's a random act of kindness you offer a stranger, the listening ear you lend a friend, the compassion you extend to those in need or those who are struggling. This warmth of yours isn't just a feeling; it's a healing force that has the power to melt away barriers and bring people together.

Embrace this warmth, let it radiate from your heart and touch the lives of those around you. Remember, in a world that can sometimes feel cold, your warmth is a precious gift. Keep letting your heart lead the way to inspire others.

DEAR UNIVERSE, my inner warmth radiates love and compassion, melting barriers and bringing comfort to all I encounter.

so be it,
so it is.

welcoming

HAVE YOU EVER NOTICED HOW YOUR open heart creates a space where others feel truly seen and accepted? Your welcoming nature is like an open door, inviting people to be their authentic selves in your presence.

This ability to make others feel at home, whether in a conversation or a crowded room, is a rare and beautiful gift. It creates connections, builds bridges, and fosters understanding. Embrace this welcoming spirit, let it guide your interactions and shape your environments. Remember, in welcoming others, you also welcome new possibilities into your own life. Open up your home and your heart to share life experiences with others.

DEAR UNIVERSE,
I radiate a welcoming energy, creating safe spaces for authenticity and fostering meaningful connections wherever I go.

so be it,
so it is.

MONTH 7

growth and learning

You either grow, or you learn. Personal development is essential for ongoing success. This month, we focus on the importance of growth and the continuous pursuit of learning.

Emphasizing growth ensures you are always evolving and adapting, which is vital for achieving and sustaining success. By embracing learning, you expand your horizons and unlock new levels of potential. Also, your soul came here to learn and to grow. This is what the magic of life is all about.

REMEMBER: Growth is a lifelong journey and it should be fun. Stay curious, seek knowledge, and watch as your growth paves the way for your manifestations.

growth

HAVE YOU EVER NOTICED HOW A TINY SEED, when nurtured, can grow into a mighty tree? You too are like that seed, brimming with beautiful potential. Every day presents an opportunity for growth, a chance to stretch your roots deeper and your branches higher. Embrace the challenges that come your way, for they are the soil in which you'll flourish. Let the rain of experience nourish you, and the sunlight of knowledge warm your spirit.

Remember, growth isn't always visible from the outside—sometimes, the most profound changes happen beneath the surface. So, tend to your inner garden with care and patience. Water your dreams with determination, prune away self-doubt, and watch as you blossom into the magnificent being you were always meant to be. Your growth is a testament to your resilience, a living masterpiece sculpted by time and perseverance. Stand tall, reach for the sky, and never stop growing.

DEAR UNIVERSE,
I am ready for growth, to stretch beyond my limits and blossom into my fullest potential. Nurture me with experiences that challenge and inspire me.

so be it,
so it is.

2

evolve

EVOLUTION IS NOT JUST FOR SPECIES OVER MILLENNIA; it's a daily choice for you. Each moment offers a crossroads—will you remain static, or will you evolve? Picture yourself as a caterpillar, comfortable in your current form, yet destined for something more. The cocoon of change may feel constricting, even frightening, but it's within this space of transformation that your true self emerges. Embrace the discomfort of shedding old beliefs and habits. Allow yourself to be reshaped by new experiences and ideas. Your evolution is not a straight line, but a spiral, revisiting familiar ground with new perspectives. As you unfold your wings, remember that every ending is a new beginning. You are constantly becoming, never finished, always evolving. Celebrate each small change, for they are the building blocks of your metamorphosis.

You're not the same person from day to day, you are on a constant journey of beautiful growth.

DEAR UNIVERSE, guide me to evolve, helping me shed what no longer serves me and embrace new growth. I am ready to unfold my wings.

so be it,
so it is.

learn

LEARNING IS THE HEARTBEAT OF A VIBRANT LIFE. It's the spark in your eyes when you grasp a new concept, the quickening of your pulse when you master a skill. Every day, the world offers you a classroom more vast than any university. Will you enroll?

A little known fact is that I didn't learn to drive until I turned thirty. I'd long avoided it, intimidated by the complexity of operating a vehicle, and my mother also was terrified of driving when I was a child, which truly impacted me. But as my life advanced, I realized I had to get outside my comfort zone and be willing to start. It's this willingness that activates the magic of learning.

Open your mind to the lessons hidden in everyday moments. Let curiosity be your compass, guiding you through uncharted territories of knowledge. Remember, learning isn't just about accumulating facts; it's about expanding your understanding of yourself and the world around you. Embrace mistakes as stepping stones, not stumbling blocks. Each error is a lesson in disguise, a chance to refine your approach. Step into the magic of a beginner's mind, always ready to question, explore, and wonder. In doing so, you'll find that the more you learn, the more you realize there is to discover. This journey of learning is lifelong, endlessly rewarding, and uniquely yours. Whether it's mastering the roads or any other skill, the key is to start and persist.

DEAR UNIVERSE, fill my days with opportunities to learn and grow. Open my mind to new ideas and experiences that enrich my understanding.

so be it, so it is.

progress

PROGRESS ISN'T ALWAYS A STRAIGHT LINE. It's more like a winding river, carving its path through the landscape of your life. Sometimes it flows swiftly, other times it seems to meander or even double back on itself. But always, always, it moves forward. Your progress is uniquely yours—don't measure it against anyone else's journey. Comparison is often said to be the thief of joy.

Celebrate the small victories, the tiny steps that add up to great distances over time. Remember, even when you feel stuck, you're gathering strength for the next surge forward. Progress is as much about the inner journey as the outer achievements. It's about becoming more of who you truly are, shedding the layers that no longer serve you. Trust in your own rhythm, your own pace. The important thing is to keep moving, keep growing, keep progressing. You are further along than you were yesterday, and that's something to be proud of.

DEAR UNIVERSE, guide my steps on the path of progress. Help me recognize and celebrate each forward move, no matter how small.

so be it,
so it is.

development

WHAT VERSION OF YOURSELF ARE YOU DEVELOPING TODAY? When I was a teenager, I studied photography and really loved to work in the darkroom, constantly developing new images of the random and abstract shots I had taken during the week. This is very similar to who you are inspired to become. Each choice you make, each action you take, adds another layer to this evolving picture. Your development is a masterpiece in progress, with infinite possibilities. Some days, you might focus on sharpening your skills, other days on broadening your perspective. Remember, development isn't just about adding new traits or abilities—it's also about refining and balancing what's already there. Be patient with yourself in this process. Just as a photograph needs time to fully develop, so do you. Embrace the journey of becoming, knowing that each stage of your development has its own beauty and purpose. You are the artist and the art, constantly creating and recreating yourself.

DEAR UNIVERSE, support me in my ongoing development. Help me shape myself into the best version I can be, day by day.

so be it, so it is.

6

enlightenment

ENLIGHTENMENT ISN'T A DESTINATION, but a journey of continuous awakening. It's the gradual lifting of the veil that separates you from deeper truths about yourself and the world around you. Imagine your mind as a beautiful sky, and enlightenment as the process of clearing away the clouds of misconception and illusion. Each moment of clarity, each flash of insight, is a ray of light breaking through. But remember, even in the clearest sky, new clouds can form.

DEAR UNIVERSE, illuminate my path toward greater understanding and enlightenment. Help me recognize and embrace the light of wisdom in all its forms.

so be it, so it is.

Enlightenment is not about achieving a permanent state of perfect understanding, but about cultivating the ability to continually seek and embrace new realizations. It's about being open to the wisdom that exists all around you—in nature, in others, and within yourself. As you walk this path, be gentle with yourself. Enlightenment comes not from forcing understanding, but from allowing it to unfold naturally. Trust in the process, and let your inner light guide you.

improvement

HOW CAN YOU BE JUST 1 PERCENT better today than you were yesterday? Improvement doesn't always come in leaps and bounds. More often, it's a series of small, consistent steps that lead to significant change over time. *Kaizen* is a Japanese word that translates to "change for the better" or "continuous improvement." It is a philosophy and set of practices focused on making small, incremental changes regularly to improve efficiency, quality, and overall performance.

Think of yourself as a sculptor, chipping away at a block of marble. Each tap of the chisel might seem insignificant, but day by day, a magnificent artwork emerges. Embrace the power of incremental progress. Celebrate the small victories—the extra rep at the gym, the moment of patience (as hard as that is) in traffic, the kind word of encouragement to a stranger. These are the building blocks of lasting improvement. Remember, the goal isn't perfection, but progress. Be kind to yourself in this journey. Improvement isn't linear; there will be setbacks and plateaus. But as long as you keep showing up, keep trying, you're improving. You're becoming a better version of yourself, one day at a time.

DEAR UNIVERSE, guide me in my journey of continuous improvement. Help me recognize and celebrate each step forward, no matter how small.

so be it, so it is.

8

advancement

PICTURE YOURSELF AS A PIONEER, constantly pushing forward into new frontiers of your own potential. Advancement is about more than just moving ahead; it's about breaking new ground, charting unexplored territories of your capabilities. Each day presents an opportunity to advance—in your skills, your understanding, your relationships, your impact on the world.

Sometimes advancement means taking bold leaps, other times it's about the steady march of consistent effort. Embrace both. Remember, advancement often requires leaving your comfort zone. It might feel uncomfortable, even scary at times, but that's where true growth happens. Celebrate each milestone, but don't rest on your laurels. There's always another horizon to reach for, another summit to climb. In advancing yourself, you also advance the world around you. Your progress ripples outward, inspiring and uplifting others. Keep moving forward, keep advancing, and watch as the world opens up before you.

DEAR UNIVERSE, propel me forward on my path of advancement. Grant me the courage to push boundaries and the wisdom to appreciate each step.

so be it,
so it is.

discovery

WHAT HIDDEN TREASURES LIE WAITING FOR you to uncover today? Life is an endless adventure of discovery, filled with wonders both great and small. Like an intrepid explorer, approach each day with a sense of curiosity and openness. The most profound discoveries often come from unexpected places—a conversation with a stranger, a detour from your usual route, a moment of quiet reflection. Be willing to question your assumptions and challenge your preconceptions. True discovery isn't just about finding new things; it's about seeing familiar things with new eyes.

This is what I have enjoyed about parenthood the most, when my children learn new things. All of their ages and stages remind me of the powerful beauty of discovery. Tasting new foods, meeting new friend groups, getting to new reading levels—there is so much joy in their discovery process.

Manifest a sense of wonder about the world around you and the world within you. Every discovery, whether it's about yourself, others, or the Universe at large, is a stepping stone to greater understanding. Embrace the joy of uncovering new truths, new beauties, new possibilities. Remember, the greatest discovery of all is the realization of your own limitless potential.

DEAR UNIVERSE, lead me to a beautiful discovery each day. Open my eyes to the wonders around and within me, guiding me to new insights.

so be it, so it is.

10

understanding

UNDERSTANDING IS THE MYSTICAL BRIDGE THAT connects us—to ourselves, to others, and to the world around us. It's more than just knowing; it's about deep comprehension that resonates in your heart as well as your mind. Like a key unlocking a door, understanding opens up new realms of possibility. Seek to understand not just with your intellect, but with empathy, energetic awareness, and compassion. Listen not just to respond but to truly hear.

Look beneath the surface, beyond the obvious, to grasp the deeper currents of meaning. Remember, understanding is a two-way street. As you strive to understand others and the world, also seek to make yourself understood. Express your thoughts, feelings, and ideas with clarity and authenticity. The more you understand, the more you realize how much there is yet to learn. Embrace this journey of ever-deepening understanding, for it is through understanding that we grow, connect, and find our place in the grand tapestry of life.

DEAR UNIVERSE, deepen my understanding of myself, others, and the world. Grant me wisdom to comprehend and compassion to connect.

so be it, so it is.

education

EDUCATION IS THE KEY THAT UNLOCKS doors to new worlds of possibility. It's not confined to classrooms or textbooks; the whole world is your school, and life itself is your greatest teacher. Approach each day with the mindset of a lifelong learner. Be curious, ask questions, seek out new experiences. Education isn't just about accumulating facts; it's about developing the ability to think critically, to see connections, to imagine new possibilities. It's about growing not just in knowledge, but in wisdom. Remember, every person you meet has something to teach you. Every challenge you face is a lesson in disguise.

Embrace both formal and informal learning opportunities. Read widely, engage in meaningful conversations, experiment with new ideas. As you educate yourself, you become better equipped to navigate life's complexities and to contribute meaningfully to the world. Your education is a gift you give yourself that keeps on giving throughout your life.

DEAR UNIVERSE, fuel my thirst for knowledge and understanding. Guide me to appreciate a love for education and experiences that expand my mind and enrich my soul.

so be it,
so it is.

12

insight

HAVE YOU EVER EXPERIENCED THAT MOMENT when suddenly, everything clicks into place? That's insight—a flash of clarity that illuminates and shines a light on the path ahead. Like a bolt of lightning in the night sky, insight can come suddenly and unexpectedly, revealing landscapes of understanding you never knew existed. But insight isn't just about those dramatic moments of revelation. It's also about the quiet realizations that come from patient observation and reflection. Practice insight by being present in each moment, by listening deeply—not just to others, but to your own inner voice.

DEAR UNIVERSE, sharpen my insight and deepen my understanding. Help me see clearly and comprehend deeply the world around and within me.

so be it, so it is.

Practice looking beneath the surface of things, questioning assumptions, and connecting seemingly unrelated dots. Remember, insight often comes when you step back and see the bigger picture. It's about perceiving patterns, understanding context, and grasping the essence of situations. As you develop your capacity for insight, you'll find yourself navigating life with greater wisdom and understanding.

knowledge

KNOWLEDGE IS THE CURRENCY OF THE MIND, the building blocks of understanding and wisdom. But it's not just about accumulating information; it's about integrating what you learn into your life in meaningful ways. Think of your mind as a vast library. Each piece of knowledge you acquire is a new book on the shelf, ready to be referenced when needed. But the true power of knowledge comes when you start making connections between these books, creating a web of understanding that's greater than the sum of its parts.

Seek knowledge widely and deeply. Be curious about everything—science, art, history, culture, nature. The more diverse your knowledge, the richer your understanding of the world becomes. Remember, knowledge isn't static. It grows, evolves, and sometimes even challenges itself. Stay open to new ideas and be willing to update your understanding as new information comes to light. Knowledge is a lifelong journey—embrace it with enthusiasm and wonder.

DEAR UNIVERSE, fill my mind with diverse and meaningful knowledge. Help me integrate what I learn to create a rich tapestry of understanding.

so be it,
so it is.

14

wisdom

I TOOK AN EVENING SWIM IN the pool the night before my daughter Lulu was born in 2015. It felt like the end of a long road after all of the miscarriages, and now it was the day before I could finally hold my soul baby in my arms. An owl appeared on the electricity cable and just stared at me. It felt like a weird transmission of wisdom that I had concluded a cycle.

Wisdom is the alchemy that transforms knowledge (and sometimes painful experiences) into understanding, information into insight. It's the ability to see beyond the surface, to grasp the deeper truths of life. Like a wise old tree that has weathered many storms, wisdom grows slowly, nourished by experience, reflection, and compassion. It's not just about knowing more, but about understanding deeply. Manifest wisdom by reflecting on your experiences, learning from your mistakes, and listening to the wisdom of others. Be open to different perspectives, for wisdom often lies in the spaces between conflicting viewpoints. Remember, true wisdom is marked by humility—the recognition that there's always more to learn. It's about asking the right questions as much as having the right answers. As you grow in wisdom, you'll find yourself navigating life's complexities with greater ease and grace, making choices that align with your deepest values and contribute to the greater good.

DEAR UNIVERSE, nurture the seeds of wisdom within me. Guide me to experiences and insights that deepen my understanding of life's profound truths.

so be it, so it is.

adaptability

ARE YOU RIGID LIKE A ROCK, worn down by the current, or flexible like a reed, bending with the flow? Adaptability is your superpower in a world of constant change. It's the ability to adjust your sails when the wind shifts, to find new paths when obstacles arise. Think of yourself as a chameleon, capable of thriving in any environment. Embrace change as an opportunity for growth rather than a threat to your comfort. Remember, adaptability isn't about losing yourself, but about finding new ways to express your essence in different contexts. It's about maintaining your core while flexing your approach. Practice stepping out of your comfort zone regularly. Try new things, meet new people, explore new ideas. The more you stretch your adaptability muscle, the stronger and more resilient you become. In a world of uncertainty, your adaptability is your greatest certainty.

DEAR UNIVERSE, grant me the adaptability to life's ever-changing currents. Help me embrace change as an opportunity for growth and transformation.

so be it, so it is.

curiosity

WHEN WAS THE LAST TIME YOU looked at the world with wonder? Curiosity is the spark that ignites the fire of learning and discovery. It's the voice that asks "why?" and "what if?" It's the drive that pushes you to explore beyond the boundaries of the known. Like a child encountering the world for the first time, approach each day with fresh eyes and an open mind. Let curiosity be your compass, guiding you to new experiences, ideas, and understandings. Ask questions, challenge assumptions, and seek out the unfamiliar. Remember, curiosity isn't just about gathering information; it's about engaging with the world in a state of active wonder. It's about being present and attentive to the marvels that surround you each and every day. Try if you can to generate curiosity in all aspects of your life—in your work, your relationships, your hobbies. The more curious you are, the richer and more vibrant your world becomes.

DEAR UNIVERSE, kindle the flame of curiosity within me. Guide me to fascinating discoveries and fill my days with wonder and excitement.

so be it, so it is.

exploration

LIFE IS AN UNCHARTED TERRITORY WAITING for you to explore. Each day is a new landscape, rich with possibilities and hidden treasures. Like an intrepid adventurer, set out with courage and excitement to discover what lies beyond the horizon of your current experience. Exploration isn't just about physical journeys; it's about venturing into new realms of thought, emotion, and understanding on a deep spiritual level. Push the boundaries of your comfort zone. Try new things, meet new people, entertain new ideas. Remember, the greatest explorers in history weren't just brave; they were also observant, patient, and open to the unexpected. As you explore, pay attention to the details, the subtle energetic shifts, the quiet revelations. Sometimes the most profound discoveries come from looking at familiar things from a new angle. Embrace the unknown, for it is in uncharted territories that you often find your true path.

DEAR UNIVERSE, ignite my spirit of exploration and guide me to new frontiers, both in the world and within myself. Fill my journey with wonder and discovery.

so be it, so it is.

18

mastery

MASTERY IS NOT A DESTINATION, but a journey of continuous refinement. It's the relentless pursuit of excellence in your chosen field, whether that's an art, a skill, or a way of being. Like a master craftsman honing their art over a lifetime, approach your pursuits with dedication and patience. My grandfather used to make violins. Imagine the precision and mastery involved with carving and assembling an instrument that creates a beautiful and resonant sound. I'm assuming that the first violin wasn't as good as the last one he created because of the mastery and skill level that is acquired with time. Just remember that we all have to begin our journey somewhere.

Embrace the process of deep practice, of making mistakes and learning from them. Remember, mastery isn't about perfection; it's about constant improvement and deepening understanding. It's about falling in love with the journey itself, finding joy in the subtle nuances and challenges of your craft. As you progress on your path to mastery, you'll find that it transforms not just your skills, but your entire approach to life. It cultivates discipline, attention to detail, and a profound appreciation for the depth and complexity of your chosen field. In pursuing mastery, you become not just better at what you do, but a better version of yourself.

DEAR UNIVERSE, guide me on the path of mastery. Grant me the patience, dedication, and insight to continually refine my skills and deepen my understanding.

so be it,
so it is.

reflection

WHEN WAS THE LAST TIME YOU truly looked within? Reflection is the mirror of the soul, offering insights that can transform your life. Like a still lake reflecting the sky, take time each day to quiet your mind and reflect on your thoughts, actions, and experiences. In the hustle of daily life, it's easy to lose touch with your inner self. But in moments of reflection, you can reconnect with your core values, reassess your goals, and realign your actions with your true purpose. Practice mindful reflection—observe your thoughts and feelings without judgment, seeking to understand rather than to criticize.

Remember, reflection isn't about dwelling on the past, but about learning from it to shape a better future. It's a powerful tool for personal growth, helping you to recognize patterns, make conscious choices, and cultivate self-awareness. In the clarity of reflection, you'll find the wisdom to navigate life's complexities with greater grace and purpose.

DEAR UNIVERSE, grant me the clarity for meaningful reflection. Help me gain insights that nurture my growth and align me with my true purpose.

so be it, so it is.

20

transformation

MY VERY FIRST SOLO ART EXHIBITION in 1999 was called *Dream of The Chrysalis*, and it was all about growth and transformation. I would draw caterpillars and butterflies going through phases of change. It's important to note you are not a fixed entity, but a being in constant transformation.

Like a caterpillar becoming a butterfly, you have the power to reinvent yourself, to shed old limitations and emerge renewed. Embrace the process of transformation, for it is through change that you grow into your fullest potential. Remember, transformation isn't always comfortable—it often requires breaking out of old patterns, facing fears, and stepping into the unknown. But it is in these moments of challenge that your true strength emerges. Trust in your ability to adapt and evolve.

DEAR UNIVERSE, guide me through the process of transformation. Help me shed what no longer serves me and embrace the emerging, authentic version of myself.

so be it,
so it is.

Visualize the person you want to become, and take small steps each day toward that vision. Transformation isn't just about changing who you are, but about revealing your authentic self, letting your inner light shine more brightly. As you transform, you inspire others to embrace their own journeys of change. You become a living testament to the incredible potential for growth that resides within each of us.

innovation

INNOVATION IS THE SPARK THAT IGNITES progress, the force that propels us into new realms of possibility. Like an inventor in their workshop, approach each day with a spirit of creativity and experimentation. Innovation isn't just about grand inventions; it's about finding new ways to solve problems, express ideas, or improve experiences. Create an innovative mindset by questioning assumptions, combining ideas in unexpected ways, and being willing to take calculated risks.

Remember, innovation often emerges from constraints and mistakes—so view challenges as opportunities to think creatively. Embrace failure as a necessary part of the innovative process, learning and iterating with each attempt. As you nurture your innovative spirit, you'll find yourself becoming more adaptable, more resilient, and more capable of navigating an ever-changing world. Your innovative thinking can ripple outward, inspiring others and contributing to the collective progress of humanity.

DEAR UNIVERSE, ignite the spark of innovation within me. Guide me to creative solutions and new ways of thinking that can positively impact the world.

so be it,
so it is.

22

breakthrough

CAN YOU FEEL IT? THAT MOMENT when everything shifts, when the impossible becomes possible? That's a breakthrough. Like a ray of sunlight breaking through storm clouds, breakthroughs illuminate new paths and possibilities. They can come in any area of life—a sudden insight that solves a problem, a moment of clarity that changes your perspective, or a surge of courage that helps you overcome a long-standing fear.

Invite the right conditions for breakthroughs by staying open, persistent, and willing to see things from new angles. Remember, breakthroughs often come after periods of struggle or seeming stagnation. Trust in the process, even when progress seems slow. Keep pushing, keep exploring, keep believing. When a breakthrough comes, embrace it fully. Let it energize and inspire you. Use it as a stepping stone to even greater achievements. Your breakthrough could be just around the corner—stay ready, stay open, and when it comes, let it propel you to new heights.

DEAR UNIVERSE, prepare me for a powerful breakthrough in all areas of my life. Grant me the insight, courage, and readiness to embrace transformative moments of change.

so be it, so it is.

skillfulness

SKILLFULNESS IS THE ART OF LIVING with grace and effectiveness. It's not just about what you do, but how you do it. Like a master musician who makes complex melodies seem effortless, practice skillfulness in all areas of your life. This means bringing mindfulness, precision, and care to everything you do—from the most mundane tasks to your greatest passions. Remember, skillfulness is developed through practice and attention. It's about continually refining your approach, learning from each experience, and always striving to improve. Be patient with yourself in this process. Skillfulness grows over time, like a tree slowly but steadily reaching for the sky. As you become more skillful, you'll find greater ease and joy in your daily life. You'll accomplish more with less effort, navigate challenges with greater finesse, and inspire others through your example. Embrace the journey of becoming ever more skillful, for it is a path of continuous growth and fulfillment.

DEAR UNIVERSE, guide me in developing skillfulness in all areas of my life. Help me approach each task with mindfulness, precision, and grace.

so be it, so it is.

24

cultivation

I GREW UP ON A 10-ACRE farm and we had over 150 avocado trees on the property. To make these beautiful avocados thrive we had to tend to them—weeding, fertilizing, and watering.

Your life is like a garden (or an orchard of avocado trees), and you are the gardener. What seeds are you planting today?

Cultivation is the deliberate nurturing of positive qualities, habits, and relationships in your life. Like a skilled gardener tending to their plants, pay attention to what you're cultivating in your thoughts, actions, and surroundings. Choose carefully what you want to grow, and tend to it with patience and care. Remember, cultivation takes time— don't expect overnight results. Instead, focus on consistent, nurturing actions. Water the seeds of your dreams with dedication, fertilize your relationships with kindness, and weed out negative influences that hinder your growth. As you grow the garden of your life, you'll find it becoming more beautiful, more abundant, and more aligned with your true self. Your cultivation efforts will not only benefit you but will also create a positive impact on those around you, as the beauty you nurture spreads and inspires others.

DEAR UNIVERSE, guide my efforts in the cultivation of a rich and fulfilling life. Help me nurture positive qualities and relationships that align with my highest good.

so be it, so it is.

expansion

HOW BIG CAN YOU DREAM? How far can you reach? Expansion is about pushing beyond your current boundaries, stretching into new territories of possibility. Like a Universe constantly growing, you too have the capacity for infinite expansion. This expansion can be in your knowledge, your skills, your impact, or your consciousness. Embrace opportunities that challenge you to grow beyond your comfort zone.

Remember, expansion often feels uncomfortable at first—it's the stretch that leads to growth. Be willing to take up space, to voice your ideas, to pursue your ambitions. As you expand, you create more room for others to grow as well. Your expansion ripples outward, inspiring and uplifting those around you. Trust in your capacity to handle greater challenges and responsibilities.

Each time you expand, you redefine what's possible for yourself and set a new baseline for future growth. Keep expanding, keep reaching, keep growing into the fullest expression of your potential.

DEAR UNIVERSE, support me in my journey of expansion. Help me stretch beyond my limits and grow into the fullest expression of my potential.

so be it,
so it is.

26

transcendence

HAVE YOU EVER FELT A MOMENT when you seemed to rise above your everyday self? I once received a powerful intuitive download that was simply three words: "rise above it." I use this when I feel overwhelmed or uncertain about the outcome of things. Transcendence is about surpassing your perceived limitations and connecting with something greater. Like an eagle soaring high above the earth, transcendence gives you a broader and clearer perspective on life. It's about moving beyond your usual thoughts, feelings, and experiences to touch something profound and transformative. Embrace moments that lift you out of the ordinary—whether through meditation, creative expression, or deep connection with others or nature. Remember, transcendence isn't about escaping reality, but about experiencing it more fully and deeply.

As you embody the essence of transcendence, you'll find yourself less bound by petty concerns and more attuned to what truly matters. You'll discover reservoirs of inner strength and wisdom you never knew you had. Let transcendence be your gateway to a more expansive, meaningful life.

DEAR UNIVERSE, guide me toward experiences of transcendence. Help me rise above my limitations and connect with the greater tapestry of existence.

so be it,
so it is.

awakening

ARE YOU TRULY AWAKE TO THE miracle of your existence? Awakening is the process of coming alive to the full spectrum of your being and the world around you and of your spiritual gifts. Like the sun rising to illuminate the world, awakening brings light to areas of your life that have been in darkness. It's about becoming conscious of your patterns, your potential, and your place in the greater web of life as a spiritual being. Embrace moments of awakening, big and small—a sudden insight, a deep connection with nature, a flash of clarity about your purpose. Remember, awakening is an ongoing journey, not a one-time event. Stay curious, stay open, and be willing to continually question your assumptions and beliefs. As you awaken, you may find that what once seemed important fades away, while new priorities emerge. Trust this process. Your awakening not only transforms your own life but can also inspire and uplift those around you, creating ripples of consciousness that extend far beyond yourself. Sometimes an awakening is mildly unpleasant as the old falls away to make space for the new, but if you bring patience and gratitude to the process, it will be a wondrous and fulfilling experience.

DEAR UNIVERSE, guide me on my journey of awakening. Help me become fully alive to the wonder of existence and conscious of my true nature.

so be it, so it is.

28

versatility

IN A WORLD OF CONSTANT CHANGE, versatility is your superpower. It's the ability to adapt, to wear many hats, to thrive in diverse situations. Like a Swiss Army knife, equipped for any situation (especially a bottle opener when you need it), cultivate a range of skills and perspectives that allow you to navigate life's varied challenges with ease. Embrace opportunities to learn new things, even if they seem unrelated to your current path—you never know when a seemingly random skill might become crucial. Remember, versatility isn't about being a jack-of-all-trades and master of none. It's about having a solid foundation that allows you to pivot and adapt as needed. It's about bringing creativity and flexibility to problem-solving. As you develop your versatility, you'll find yourself becoming more resilient, more confident in your ability to handle whatever life throws your way. You'll discover new passions, new strengths, and new ways of expressing your unique gifts in the world.

DEAR UNIVERSE, nurture my versatility and adaptability. Help me develop a diverse range of skills and perspectives to navigate life's challenges with grace.

so be it,
so it is.

realization

REALIZATION IS THE MOMENT WHEN KNOWLEDGE becomes understanding, when concepts crystallize into clarity. It's the "aha!" moment that changes everything. Like a fog lifting to reveal a breathtaking landscape, realization brings sudden clarity and new perspective. These moments of realization can come in any area of life—a deep insight about yourself, a new understanding of a relationship, or a flash of clarity about your purpose. Be open to these moments of realization. Create space for them by reflecting, questioning, and staying curious. Remember, realization often comes when you least expect it—in moments of quiet, or through seemingly unrelated experiences.

When a realization dawns, sit with it. Let it sink in. Allow it to reshape your understanding and inform your actions. Each realization is a stepping stone on your path of growth and self-discovery. Embrace these moments of clarity, for they are the signposts guiding you toward your truest, most authentic life.

DEAR UNIVERSE, open my mind and heart to a profound realization. Guide me to insights that deepen my understanding and align me with my highest truth.

so be it,
so it is.

30

flourishing

IMAGINE YOURSELF AS A VIBRANT VASE of flowers in full bloom, each aspect of your life a different flower contributing to the overall beauty. Flourishing is about thriving in all dimensions—mentally, emotionally, physically, and spiritually. It's not just about surviving, but about living with vitality, purpose, and joy. Like a well-tended flower garden, flourishing requires care, attention, and the right conditions. Nurture your mind with continuous learning, your body with healthy habits, your spirit with meaningful practices, and your heart with loving relationships. Remember, flourishing doesn't mean the absence of challenges—even the most beautiful gardens face storms. It's about having the resilience to weather difficulties and the ability to find growth opportunities in every situation. As you flourish, you naturally inspire and uplift those around you. Your vitality becomes contagious, your joy infectious. Embrace the journey of flourishing, for in your thriving, you contribute to the flourishing of the world.

DEAR UNIVERSE, support me in flourishing in all aspects of my life. Help me cultivate the conditions for vibrant growth and joyful living.

so be it, so it is.

self-improvement

THE JOURNEY OF SELF-IMPROVEMENT IS THE most important voyage you'll ever undertake. It's a lifelong expedition of discovering your potential, overcoming limitations, and becoming the best version of yourself. Like an incredible artist using bold strokes and layers of paint on a canvas to create a beautiful landscape, approach your self-improvement with the same level of creativity, patience, persistence, and self-compassion. Set meaningful goals, but remember that true self-improvement is about the journey, not just the destination. Embrace challenges as opportunities for growth, view setbacks as valuable lessons, and celebrate your progress, no matter how small. Remember, self-improvement isn't about becoming someone else—it's about becoming more authentically yourself. It's about aligning your actions with your values, cultivating your strengths, and transforming your weaknesses into opportunities for growth. As you commit to self-improvement, you'll find that your growth positively impacts every aspect of your life and inspires others to embark on their own journeys of personal development.

DEAR UNIVERSE, guide me on my journey of self-improvement. Help me uncover my potential, overcome limitations, and become the best version of myself.

so be it, so it is.

MONTH 8

peace and tranquility

Imagine your inner world is as tranquil and still as it can possibly be. Inner peace is crucial for clear thinking and emotional stability. This month, we concentrate on creating a serene mind and manifesting mindfulness.

Achieving peace allows for better decision-making and maintaining focus on your goals. By nurturing tranquility, you enhance your emotional resilience and mental clarity.

REMEMBER: Peace is the bedrock of a focused mind and a balanced soul. Cultivate calm, embrace the essence of tranquility, and see how your goals become more attainable with a clear and peaceful mind.

serenity

IN THE MIDST OF LIFE'S CHAOS, have you found your inner sanctuary? Serenity is not the absence of storms, but the calm within them. Picture yourself as a tranquil lake, reflecting the sky above, unmoved by the winds that ripple your surface. This inner peace is always within you, waiting to be accessed. Embrace the energy of serenity by creating moments of stillness in your day. Take deep breaths, letting each exhale carry away tension. Practice mindfulness, anchoring yourself in the present moment. Remember, serenity is a choice—a way of responding to life rather than reacting to it. It's about accepting what you cannot change and finding peace in that acceptance. As you nurture your inner serenity, you'll find yourself better equipped to handle life's challenges with grace and equanimity. Let your serenity be a beacon of peace for others, inspiring calm in those around you.

DEAR UNIVERSE, fill my heart with serenity and help me invite inner peace amid life's storms. Guide me to be a source of calm for myself and others.

so be it,
so it is.

2

calm

HAVE YOU EVER BEEN TOLD TO CALM DOWN? Isn't it ironic how it usually has the opposite effect? Don't you dare tell me to calm down.

Calm is your superpower in a world of constant stimulation. Like a deep, still ocean beneath turbulent waves, your inner calm remains undisturbed by surface agitations. Welcome this calm by creating pockets of quiet in your day. Turn off notifications, step away from screens, and allow yourself moments of uninterrupted peace. Practice deep breathing, feeling each inhale bring in tranquility and each exhale release tension. Remember, calm is not about suppressing emotions, but about responding to them with mindful awareness. It's about creating space between stimulus and response, allowing you to choose your reactions wisely.

As you nurture your inner calm, you'll find yourself more centered, more focused, and better able to navigate life's ups and downs with grace. Let your calm presence be a soothing balm for those around you, creating an oasis of peace wherever you go.

DEAR UNIVERSE, infuse my being with deep, abiding calm. Help me maintain inner peace amid outer turbulence, radiating tranquility to all around me.

so be it, so it is.

peace

WHAT DOES PEACE MEAN TO YOU? Is it a state of being, a way of living, or both? Peace is not just the absence of conflict, but the presence of harmony—within yourself and with the world around you. Imagine yourself as a peaceful garden, where diverse elements such as roses and cacti coexist in beautiful balance. Nurture inner peace by aligning your thoughts, words, and actions with your deepest values. Practice forgiveness—of yourself and others—letting go of resentments that disturb your tranquility.

Remember, peace is not passive; it requires active nurturing. It's about choosing love over fear (always), understanding over judgment, and compassion over indifference. As you invite peace within, you naturally become a peacemaker in your relationships and communities. Your peaceful presence can ripple outward, touching lives in ways you may never fully know. Embrace peace as a way of being, and watch as it transforms your world from the inside out.

DEAR UNIVERSE, fill my heart with peace and guide my actions to create harmony within and around me. Let me be an instrument of peace in the world.

so be it, so it is.

4

tranquility

AN ALARM WAS GOING OFF AT the airport one day and I was praying for tranquility. Kids were screaming, we were at the gate waiting to board and this screeching noise just would not stop. And then finally after at least thirty minutes with our fingers in our ears, it did. There's a powerful reminder in the contrast, that the calm can sometimes come after the storm.

Tranquility is the gentle whisper of your soul amid the noise of the world. Like a serene mountain lake reflecting the sky, your tranquil mind mirrors the vastness of inner peace. Embrace tranquility by simplifying your life—declutter your space, streamline your schedule, and prioritize what truly matters. Create rituals that bring you back to center—perhaps a morning meditation, an evening walk, or moments of mindful breathing throughout the day.

DEAR UNIVERSE, envelop me in tranquility, guiding me to inner stillness amid life's movements. Help me radiate peaceful energy to all I encounter.

so be it,
so it is.

Remember, tranquility is not about escaping life's challenges, but about meeting them with a calm and centered presence. It's about finding stillness within motion, silence within sound. As you nurture your inner tranquility, you'll find yourself more resilient, more intuitive, and more in tune with the natural flow of life. Let your tranquil presence be a sanctuary for others, offering a space of calm in a hectic world.

quietude

IN 2023, MY HOME IN SAG HARBOR backed onto the woods. My phone was blowing up with work calls and family issues, so I left it behind and decided to go for a walk. The deeper I got into the woods, the quieter it became. Surrounded by the comforting presence of the trees, I felt so free knowing that no one knew where I was and no one could reach me. It was a sublime manifestation of quietude.

Quietude is not just the absence of noise, but the presence of a deep, nurturing silence. Practice quietude by creating spaces of silence in your day—turn off the TV, put away your phone, perhaps walk into the woods and simply be. Practice listening—not just to others, but to the subtle voices of nature, your body, and your innermost self. Remember, quietude is not about suppressing your voice, but about tuning in to the wisdom that speaks in silence. It's about finding the stillness between words, the pauses between breaths and the hustle of thoughts. As you embrace quietude, you'll discover a richness in silence that no words can capture. You'll find yourself more attuned to the subtle rhythms of life, more present in each moment. Let your quiet presence speak volumes, inspiring others to discover the power of stillness.

DEAR UNIVERSE, immerse me in the nurturing embrace of quietude. Help me find wisdom in silence and peace in stillness.

so be it,
so it is.

harmony

HARMONY IS THE BEAUTIFUL DANCE OF diverse elements coming together in perfect balance. Like a well-designed room where each piece of furniture enhances the overall space, you too can practice harmony in your life. In feng shui, the ancient Chinese art of placement, every object has its ideal position to promote positive energy flow. The sturdy dining table anchors the room, fostering connection and nourishment. Comfortable seating invites relaxation and conversation, while carefully placed lighting creates ambiance and functionality. Even empty spaces play a crucial role, allowing energy to circulate freely.

Start by aligning your thoughts, words, and actions—let them work in unison like a thoughtfully arranged living space. Find balance between work and rest, giving and receiving, speaking and listening. Remember, harmony doesn't mean the absence of discord; it's about integrating all aspects of life into a coherent whole. Embrace the challenges as necessary contrasts, the quiet moments as essential breathing room.

As you nurture harmony within yourself, you'll naturally create it in your environment and relationships. You'll move through life with a sense of flow and grace, attuned to the energies around you. Let your harmonious presence inspire others to find their own inner balance and contribute to the grand design of life.

DEAR UNIVERSE, guide me to create harmony in all aspects of my life. Help me balance different elements and flow in sync with life's rhythms.

so be it, so it is.

stillness

HAVE YOU EVER TRULY EXPERIENCED THE power of stillness? In a world that glorifies constant motion, stillness is a revolutionary act. Like a deep, clear pool reflecting the sky, your still mind reflects the vastness of your inner being. Practice stillness through meditation, mindful breathing, or simply sitting in quiet awareness. Create pockets of stillness in your day—a moment of pause before reacting, a breath of silence before speaking. Remember, stillness is not about doing nothing; it's about being fully present in the moment.

It's in stillness that you can hear your inner wisdom, connect with your true self, and tap into the infinite potential within you. When you embrace stillness, you'll find yourself moving through life with greater clarity, purpose, and peace. Your still presence will become a sanctuary for others, inviting them to discover their own inner calm.

DEAR UNIVERSE, immerse me in the transformative power of stillness. Help me find clarity, wisdom, and peace in moments of quiet presence.

so be it, so it is.

8

relaxation

RELAXATION IS NOT A LUXURY, but a necessity for your well-being. Picture yourself as a flower, gently unfurling its petals in the warm sunlight. This is the essence of relaxation—a natural state of openness and ease. Embrace the energy of relaxation by creating rituals that help you unwind—a warm bath, gentle stretches, or simply lying on the grass and watching clouds drift by. Practice progressive muscle relaxation, tensing and then releasing each part of your body.

Remember, relaxation is not about being lazy; it's about releasing tension and restoring balance. It's in this state of relaxation that your body heals, your mind clears, and your spirit rejuvenates. When you lean into prioritizing relaxation, you'll find yourself more productive, more creative, and more alive. Your relaxed presence will be a gentle reminder to others to slow down and savor life's moments.

DEAR UNIVERSE, envelop me in deep relaxation, releasing tension from my body and mind. Guide me to balance activity with restorative rest.

*so be it,
so it is.*

soothing

IN A WORLD THAT CAN OFTEN feel harsh and abrasive, be a soothing presence—for yourself and others. Like a gentle stream smoothing rough stones, let your energy soften the sharp edges of life. Create a soothing environment around you—soft lighting, calming colors, gentle sounds. Practice self-soothing techniques like deep breathing, positive self-talk, or gently stroking your arm.

Remember, soothing is not about avoiding difficult emotions, but about comforting yourself through them. There's a subtle yet beautiful power to treating yourself with the same kindness you'd offer a dear friend. As you nurture this soothing energy, you'll find yourself more resilient in the face of stress and more compassionate toward others' struggles.

Your soothing presence will be a balm for weary souls, offering comfort and calm in a chaotic world.

DEAR UNIVERSE, infuse my being with soothing energy. Help me comfort myself and others, spreading gentleness and calm wherever I go.

so be it, so it is.

10

contentment

CONTENTMENT IS THE ART OF FINDING joy in what you have, rather than yearning for what you lack. Like a tree firmly rooted in the earth, drawing nourishment from where it stands, you too can find fulfillment in your present circumstances. Nourish the energy of contentment by practicing gratitude—regularly acknowledge the blessings in your life, big and small. Find pleasure in simple things—a warm cup of tea, a beautiful sunset, a kind word from a friend. Remember, contentment doesn't mean complacency; it's about appreciating your journey while still growing and evolving. It's about finding peace in the present moment while holding space for future dreams.

DEAR UNIVERSE,
fill my heart with
contentment and
gratitude for all
that I am and have.
Help me find joy in
the present while
embracing growth.

so be it,
so it is.

As you nurture contentment, you'll find a deep sense of inner peace and joy that isn't dependent on external circumstances. Your contented presence will inspire others to find satisfaction in their own lives, creating a ripple effect of joy and gratitude.

restfulness

IN A WORLD THAT OFTEN EQUATES busyness with importance, embrace the power of restfulness. Like a field lying fallow, regenerating its nutrients, you too need periods of rest to replenish your energy and creativity. Create a restful environment in your home—a cozy corner for reading, a comfortable bed for good sleep. Practice good sleep rituals, establishing a soothing bedtime routine. Remember, restfulness is not just about physical sleep; it's also about mental and emotional relaxation. Give yourself permission to take breaks, to do nothing, to simply be.

As you prioritize restfulness, you'll find yourself more energized, more focused, and more emotionally balanced. Your well-rested presence will remind others of the importance of slowing down and recharging. In restfulness, you're not just recovering—you're preparing for your next phase of growth and creativity.

DEAR UNIVERSE, envelop me in deep restfulness. Guide me to balance activity with rejuvenation, nurturing my body, mind, and spirit.

so be it, so it is.

12

solace

IN CHAPTERS OF OUR LIVES WHERE we are navigating change, seeking solace is imperative. In moments of stillness, I seek solace in the gentle embrace of the Universe, trusting its boundless wisdom and infinite love. In life's challenging moments, can you find solace within yourself? Solace is the comfort you give to your own soul, a gentle balm for your wounds. Like a sheltered cove in a stormy sea, create a space of solace within your heart. Embody the energy of self-compassion, treating yourself with the same kindness you'd offer a dear friend. Develop rituals that bring you comfort—perhaps lighting a candle, listening to soothing music, or wrapping yourself in a soft blanket. Remember, seeking solace is not a sign of weakness, but an act of self-care and inner strength. It's about acknowledging your pain while also nurturing your resilience.

As you learn to provide solace for yourself, you'll become better equipped to offer comfort to others. Your ability to find peace amid difficulties will inspire those around you, showing that even in the darkest times, solace can be found.

DEAR UNIVERSE, wrap me in the warm embrace of solace. Help me find inner comfort and strength, becoming a source of peace for myself and others.

so be it,
so it is.

gentle

IN A WORLD THAT OFTEN VALUES TOUGHNESS, defensiveness, and being "ballsy," dare to be gentle. Gentleness is not weakness; it's strength wrapped in kindness. Like a soft breeze that can eventually wear down tall mountains, your gentle presence can create profound change. Practice gentleness in your thoughts, replacing harsh self-criticism with compassionate understanding. Extend this gentleness to your actions, moving through the world with care and consideration. Speak gently, choosing words that heal rather than hurt. Remember, gentleness doesn't mean being a pushover or a people pleaser; it's about responding to life with grace and empathy. It's about handling yourself, others, and the world with tender care.

As you invite gentleness, you'll find your relationships deepening, your impact softening yet strengthening. Your gentle presence will be a soothing essence in a world that often feels too harsh, inspiring others to approach life with more kindness and care.

DEAR UNIVERSE, infuse my being with gentle energy. Guide me to interact with myself and others with tender care and compassionate strength.

so be it,
so it is.

14

softness

IN A WORLD THAT CAN FEEL hard and unyielding, embrace the power of softness. Softness is not about being weak or pliable, but about being receptive and adaptive. Like water that can wear down stone, your softness is a form of strength. Embody the essence of softness in your approach to life—be open to new ideas, flexible in your expectations, and gentle in your judgments. Practice soft focus, allowing your gaze and your mind to relax and expand. Remember, softness is not about losing your form, but about finding resilience through flexibility. It's about meeting resistance with receptivity, tension with tenderness. As you embrace softness, you'll find yourself more adaptable to life's changes, more open to its lessons. Your soft presence will be a welcome relief in a world that often feels too rigid, inviting others to soften their own edges and approach life with more fluidity and grace.

DEAR UNIVERSE, imbue my being with softness. Help me approach life with flexibility and openness, finding strength in gentleness and adaptation.

so be it,
so it is.

DAY

15

ease

WHAT IF LIFE COULD FLOW WITH MORE EASE? Ease is not about avoiding challenges, but about moving through them with grace and fluidity. Imagine yourself as a little leaf floating down a stream, navigating rocks and rapids with natural buoyancy. Manifest the energy of ease by releasing resistance to what is—accept your current circumstances while working toward change. Simplify your life, decluttering your space and schedule to create more breathing room. Practice going with the flow, trusting in the natural unfolding of events.

Remember, ease doesn't mean laziness or passivity; it's about aligning yourself with the current of life rather than constantly swimming upstream. It's about finding the path of least resistance while still moving toward your goals. As you embrace ease, you'll find yourself accomplishing more with less struggle, enjoying the journey as much as the destination. Your ease-filled presence will inspire others to release unnecessary struggle and find more flow in their own lives.

DEAR UNIVERSE, guide me to a state of ease in all aspects of my life. Help me flow with life's currents, accomplishing with grace and joy.

so be it, so it is.

bliss

HAVE YOU TOUCHED MOMENTS OF PURE bliss in your life? Bliss is not just fleeting happiness, but a deep state of joy and contentment that arises from within. Like a wellspring of joy bubbling up from your core, bliss is your natural state when you're aligned with your true self. Nurture blissful energy by doing things that make your soul sing—whether that's creating art, helping others, or simply basking in nature's beauty. Practice mindfulness to fully immerse yourself in blissful moments, savoring them with all your senses. Remember, bliss is not about constant euphoria, but about finding joy even amid life's challenges. The power of the pause can never be underestimated.

It's about connecting with the inherent beauty and wonder of existence. As you nurture your capacity for bliss, you'll find yourself more resilient, more grateful, and more alive. Your blissful presence will be contagious, uplifting those around you and reminding them of the joy available in each moment.

DEAR UNIVERSE, awaken the wellspring of bliss within me. Guide me to moments of pure joy and help me radiate this blissful energy to others.

so be it, so it is.

composure

IN THE FACE OF LIFE'S STORMS, can you maintain your composure? Composure is the art of staying centered and calm, regardless of external circumstances. Like a deeply rooted tree standing firm in strong winds, your composure is your anchor in turbulent times. Practice composure by developing a strong inner core—nurture your values, build your self-confidence, and practice emotional regulation. In times of struggle, feel your feet firmly planted on the ground. Stand tall and focus on your gift of breathing in each moment that passes.

When faced with challenges, always reconnect with your center before responding. As you strengthen your composure, you'll find yourself better equipped to handle life's ups and downs with dignity and grace. Your composed presence will be a stabilizing force for those around you, inspiring calm and confidence in turbulent times.

DEAR UNIVERSE, strengthen my inner core and help me maintain composure in all situations. Guide me to respond with grace and calm under pressure.

so be it, so it is.

placid

HAVE YOU EVER EXPERIENCED SITTING ON the beach at night with the fog rolling in? One evening in Montauk, the Atlantic Ocean's silvery waters were almost perfectly calm. The scene was so placid that it felt otherworldly.

In a world of constant motion and noise, set the intention to have a placid spirit. Placidity is like a still lake, unruffled by passing winds, reflecting the sky in perfect clarity. Create moments of placidity in your day—perhaps a quiet morning ritual or an evening wind-down routine. Practice letting thoughts and worries float by without engaging them, like clouds reflected on a calm lake surface. Remember, being placid doesn't mean being passive or emotionless.

It's about finding a place of inner quiet from which you can engage with the world more effectively. It's about maintaining a sense of perspective amid life's dramas. As you nurture your placid nature, you'll find yourself less reactive, more thoughtful, and better able to navigate life's challenges. Your placid presence will be a soothing influence on those around you, creating an atmosphere of calm wherever you go.

DEAR UNIVERSE, infuse my spirit with placid energy. Help me maintain inner calm and clarity, becoming a source of peace in a turbulent world.

so be it,
so it is.

zen

EMBRACE THE ZEN WAY OF BEING—fully present, unburdened by past or future. Like a Zen garden, simple yet profound, cultivate a mind that is clear, orderly, and deeply peaceful. Practice mindfulness in everyday activities—feel the water on your hands as you wash dishes, savor each bite of your meal, fully engage in conversations. Simplify your life, letting go of what's unnecessary to make space for what truly matters. Remember, Zen is not about achieving a particular state, but about being fully awake to each moment as it is.

It's about finding the extraordinary in the ordinary, the sacred in the mundane. As you practice a Zen approach to life, you'll find yourself more grounded, more aware, and more in tune with the flow of existence. Your Zen-like presence will inspire others to slow down, pay attention, and find deeper meaning in their daily lives.

DEAR UNIVERSE, guide me toward a Zen state of being. Help me live fully in each moment, finding peace and profound meaning in simplicity.

so be it, so it is.

20

serene

SERENITY IS YOUR BIRTHRIGHT—CLAIM IT. Like a majestic mountain unmoved by passing clouds, invite an inner serenity that remains steady amid life's fluctuations. Create a serene environment around you—declutter your space, surround yourself with calming colors and textures, let in natural light. Practice serenity in your interactions, responding to conflicts with calm understanding rather than heated emotion.

DEAR UNIVERSE, envelop me in deep serene energy. Help me maintain inner peace amid outer turbulence, radiating calm to all I encounter.

so be it, so it is.

Remember, serenity is not about avoiding life's challenges, but about meeting them with a peaceful heart and a clear mind.

It's about finding stillness within movement, silence within sound. As you nurture your serenity, you'll find yourself better able to navigate life's complexities with grace and wisdom. Your serene presence will be a balm for those around you, creating an oasis of peace in a chaotic world.

mild

IN A WORLD THAT OFTEN CELEBRATES INTENSITY, embrace the power of mildness. Like a gentle spring day, your mild presence can be deeply refreshing and nurturing. Practice mildness in your speech, choosing words that soothe rather than inflame. Practice mild responses to things that trigger you, diffusing tension with calm understanding. Create a mild atmosphere in your home, with soft lighting, gentle scents, and soothing textures. Remember, being mild doesn't mean being weak or ineffective.

It's about approaching life with gentleness and consideration, creating harmony rather than discord. It's about tempering strength with kindness, power with compassion. As you embrace mildness, you'll find your relationships improving and your impact deepening. Your mild presence will be a welcome relief in a harsh world, inspiring others to approach life with more gentleness and care.

DEAR UNIVERSE, infuse my being with a mild energy. Guide me to interact with the world gently and considerately, creating harmony wherever I go.

so be it, so it is.

DAY 22

repose

IN THE MIDST OF LIFE'S DEMANDS, can you find moments of repose? Repose is more than rest—it's a state of serene tranquility. Like a cat basking in a sunbeam, fully relaxed yet quietly alert, cultivate the art of deep repose. Create a space in your home dedicated to repose—a comfortable chair, a meditation cushion, or a cozy nook. Practice active relaxation techniques like progressive muscle relaxation or different forms of meditation.

Remember, repose is not about escaping your responsibilities, but about recharging so you can meet them more effectively. It's about finding stillness within activity, relaxation within engagement. As you nurture your capacity for repose, you'll find yourself more resilient, more creative, and more attuned to life's subtle joys. Your reposed presence will remind others of the importance of deep relaxation in a world that often glorifies busyness.

DEAR UNIVERSE, guide me to states of deep repose. Help me find tranquility amid activity, rejuvenating my body, mind, and spirit.

so be it,
so it is.

restful

EMBRACE THE RESTORATIVE POWER OF RESTFULNESS. Like a garden replenishing itself overnight, your body and mind need periods of deep rest to flourish. Create a sleep sanctuary in your bedroom—comfortable bedding, cool temperature, and darkness. Develop a restful bedtime routine—perhaps gentle stretching, reading a calming book, or listening to soothing music. Practice restfulness throughout your day with short breaks, deep breathing, or brief meditations.

Remember, being restful is not about being inactive, but about balancing activity with recovery. It's about giving yourself permission to pause, to recharge, to simply be. As you prioritize restfulness, you'll find yourself more energized, more focused, and more emotionally balanced. Your restful presence will inspire others to value and prioritize their own rest and recovery.

DEAR UNIVERSE, envelop me in restful energy. Guide me to balance activity with rejuvenation, nurturing my well-being on all levels.

*so be it,
so it is.*

24

silent

IN A WORLD FULL OF NOISE, discover the power of silence. Silence is not just the absence of sound, but a presence in itself—rich, deep, and transformative. Like a snow-covered landscape absorbing all sound, create moments of profound silence in your day. Practice silent meditation, allowing thoughts to settle like snow falling softly to the ground. Engage in silent activities—walking in nature, creating art, or simply sitting in quiet contemplation.

DEAR UNIVERSE, immerse me in the transformative power of silent energy. Help me find wisdom in quiet moments and speak from a place of inner stillness.

so be it, so it is.

Remember, embracing silence doesn't mean you never speak; it's about speaking from a place of inner quiet, with words that truly matter. It's about listening deeply—to others, to nature, to your own inner voice. As you practice silence, you'll find your mind clearing, your intuition sharpening, and your presence deepening. Your silent presence will speak volumes, inviting others into a space of peaceful reflection.

smooth

LIFE DOESN'T HAVE TO BE ROUGH—set the intention for smoothness in your journey. Like the pebble polished by the river, let your experiences smooth away your rough edges. Practice moving through your day with fluid grace—in your physical movements, in your interactions, in your problem-solving. Create smooth transitions between activities, allowing one moment to flow seamlessly into the next. Remember, smoothness doesn't mean avoiding all obstacles; it's about navigating them with minimal friction and maximum adaptability.

It's about finding the path of least resistance while still moving toward your goals. As you embrace smoothness, you'll find yourself moving through life with more ease and less stress. Your smooth presence will be a calming influence, showing others how to navigate life's complexities with grace and fluidity.

DEAR UNIVERSE, guide me toward embodying smooth energy in all aspects of my life. Help me move with fluid grace, navigating challenges with ease and adaptability.

so be it,
so it is.

26

subdued

LIKE THE SOFT LIGHT OF DAWN, your subdued presence can be deeply comforting and transformative. Embrace a subdued demeanor—speak softly, move gently, listen deeply. Create a subdued environment that soothes the senses—soft colors, gentle textures, subtle scents. Practice subdued self-expression, letting your actions speak louder than your words. Remember, being subdued doesn't mean being invisible or ineffective. It's about having a quiet confidence, a gentle strength that doesn't need to announce itself.

It's about making an impact through depth rather than volume. As you embrace a more subdued way of being, you'll find yourself having a profound influence on those around you. Your subdued presence will be a welcome relief in a noisy world, inviting others into a space of calm reflection and genuine connection.

> **DEAR UNIVERSE,** infuse my being with subdued grace. Help me impact the world gently yet profoundly, radiating quiet strength and deep peace.
>
> *so be it, so it is.*

tender

TENDERNESS IS NOT WEAKNESS; it's the courage to remain openhearted. Like a new leaf unfurling in spring, cultivate a tender approach to life. Practice self-compassion, treating yourself with gentle kindness. Extend this tenderness to others, approaching their vulnerabilities with care and understanding. Create tender moments in your day—a gentle touch, a kind word, a compassionate thought. Remember, being tender doesn't mean being a pushover; it's about combining strength with gentleness, courage with compassion.

It's about handling the world, others, and yourself with loving care. As you nurture tenderness, you'll find your connections deepening and your impact softening yet strengthening. Your tender presence will be a healing balm, reminding others of the transformative power of gentleness and compassion.

DEAR UNIVERSE, awaken deep and tender energy within me. Guide me to approach life, others, and myself with gentle strength and compassionate care.

so be it,
so it is.

28

surrender

ALL OF THE SCRIPTURES FROM THE world's major faiths mention the power of surrender. What might change if you surrendered to the flow of life? Surrender is not about giving up, but about letting go of resistance. Like a leaf carried by the wind, trust in the gusts of life to guide you. Practice surrendering control—release your grip on outcomes and trust in the unfolding of events. Trust in the energy of acceptance of what is, even as you work toward what could be. Remember, surrender is not passive; it's an active alignment with the greater flow of existence.

It's about co-creating with life rather than struggling against it. As you embrace surrender, you'll find yourself moving through life with more ease and grace. Your surrendered presence will inspire others to release unnecessary struggle and find peace in acceptance.

DEAR UNIVERSE,
guide me to a state of wise surrender. Help me release resistance and trust in the flow of life, finding peace in acceptance.

so be it,
so it is.

wholeness

YOU ARE ALREADY WHOLE—can you recognize and embrace this truth? Wholeness is not something to achieve, but to uncover. Like a perfect circle, complete in itself, you are inherently whole. Practice self-acceptance, embracing all aspects of yourself—light and shadow, strengths and weaknesses. Invite integration in your life, balancing different aspects of your being—work and play, solitude and connection, action and rest.

Remember, wholeness doesn't mean perfection; it's about embracing your full humanity, your completeness just as you are. It's about healing the illusion of separation and recognizing your interconnectedness with all of life. As you embody wholeness, you'll find a deep sense of peace and authenticity. Your whole presence will inspire others to embrace their own completeness and live from a place of integrated authenticity.

DEAR UNIVERSE, awaken me to my inherent wholeness. Help me embrace all aspects of myself, living from a place of integrated authenticity.

so be it, so it is.

30

mellow

EMBRACE THE ART OF BEING MELLOW—SOFT, smooth, and free from harshness. Like a warm sunset casting a golden glow, let your mellow presence soothe and uplift. Embody the essence of a relaxed attitude toward life's ups and downs, maintaining equanimity in the face of challenges. Create a mellow atmosphere around you—soft music, warm lighting, comfortable surroundings. Practice mellow interactions, approaching others with easygoing warmth and gentle humor.

DEAR UNIVERSE,
infuse my being with mellow energy. Guide me to approach life with relaxed warmth, bringing ease and joy to every moment.

so be it,
so it is.

Remember, being mellow doesn't mean being apathetic or disengaged. It's about engaging with life from a place of relaxed alertness, responding rather than reacting. It's about bringing a sense of ease and warmth to your experiences and interactions. As you embrace mellowness, you'll find yourself navigating life with more grace and less stress. Your mellow presence will be a calming influence, inviting others to relax and find joy in the present moment.

tranquil

IN THE MIDST OF LIFE'S CHAOS, be a sanctuary of tranquility. Tranquility is not just calmness, but a deep, abiding peace that weathers all storms. Like a serene lake reflecting the sky, cultivate inner stillness that mirrors the vastness of your true nature. Create tranquil spaces in your home and in your day—moments of quiet reflection, peaceful rituals, serene environments.

Practice tranquility in your thoughts, letting worries and anxieties float away like clouds in a clear sky. Remember, tranquility is not about avoiding life's challenges, but about meeting them from a place of inner peace. It's about maintaining a calm center even when the surface is rippled. As you nurture tranquility, you'll find yourself moving through life with greater ease and clarity. Your tranquil presence will be a haven for others, offering a space of peace in a turbulent world.

DEAR UNIVERSE, envelop me in deep tranquil energy. Help me maintain inner peace amid outer turbulence, becoming a sanctuary of calm for myself and others.

so be it, so it is.

MONTH 9

creativity and inspiration

The Universe is always flowing through you with the energy and truest essence of creativity and inspiration. Encouraging creativity is vital for innovation and problem-solving and the manifestation of life-force energy. This month, we inspire you to tap into your creative potential and find new sources of inspiration.

Sparking creativity helps you think outside the box and approach challenges with fresh perspectives. By seeking inspiration, you ignite your passion and drive.

REMEMBER: Creativity unlocks new possibilities and manifests magic. Embrace your creative side, seek inspiration, and watch as your innovative ideas lead you to success.

creation

HAVE YOU EVER PAUSED TO MARVEL at the miracle of your own existence? You are a living, breathing work of art, sculpted by the cosmos itself. Each cell in your body is a Universe unto itself, teeming with infinite potential and purpose. As you move through life, remember that you are not just observing creation—you are creation itself, unfolding in real time. Your thoughts, actions, and choices ripple out into the world, shaping reality in ways both seen and unseen. Embrace your role as a co-creator of your destiny. With every breath, you have the power to bring something new into being. What will you choose to create and manifest today?

DEAR UNIVERSE,
I am a vessel of boundless creativity, channeling the cosmic force of creation through my very being. Guide my hands and heart as I shape my reality.

so be it,
so it is.

2

inspire

YOU ARE A BEACON OF LIGHT in a world that sometimes feels shrouded in darkness. Your words, your actions, your very presence have the power to ignite the spark of hope in others. Think of a time when someone's kindness or courage inspired you to be better, to reach higher, to persevere. Now, imagine yourself as that source of inspiration for others.

Every smile you share, every act of compassion you perform, every challenge you overcome—these are the brushstrokes that paint a more beautiful world. Your life is a masterpiece in progress, and those around you draw strength from your example. Dare to shine brightly, for in doing so, you give others permission to do the same.

DEAR UNIVERSE,
I am a radiant source of energy that has the power to inspire others. May I uplift those around me with my words, actions, and energy. May my light kindle the flames of hope in others.

so be it,
so it is.

imagine

CLOSE YOUR EYES AND LET YOUR mind wander beyond the boundaries of what is known. In the realm of imagination, you are limitless. Here, mountains can be moved with a thought, and new worlds spring into being with a whisper. Your imagination is the seedbed of all that is possible—the birthplace of inventions, art, and solutions yet to be discovered. When you unleash the full power of your imagination, you tap into the same creative force that birthed the cosmos.

What wild dreams lie dormant within you, waiting to be awakened? What impossible things might become possible if you dared to imagine them into existence? Today (and all days), give yourself permission to dream bigger than ever before.

DEAR UNIVERSE, my imagination is a gateway to infinite possibilities. I open my mind to imagine and receive visions of beauty, innovation, and wonder beyond my wildest dreams.

so be it, so it is.

4

innovation

MY SPEAKING CAREER WAS ON THE verge of taking off. I was booked for at least three highly paid keynote gigs when the pandemic of 2020 stopped the world in its tracks. In-person meetings, events, even school came to a complete standstill. We had no choice but to innovate. That's when the rise of Zoom and hosting online events became a necessity. We had to pivot to keep the business in operation and also profitable.

In a world of constant change, your ability to innovate is your greatest asset. Innovation isn't just about creating new gadgets or technologies—it's a mindset, a way of approaching life with curiosity and openness. Every problem you encounter is an invitation to think differently, to challenge the status quo, to find a better way. Look around you. What could be improved? What needs could be met in a new way? Your unique perspective and experiences give you the power to see solutions where others see only obstacles.

> **DEAR UNIVERSE,**
> I am a wellspring of ideas for innovation, constantly seeking new ways to improve the world around me. Guide me toward creative solutions that benefit all.
>
> *so be it,*
> *so it is.*

artistry

WHEN I WAS A LITTLE GIRL I grew up in galleries and studios around the world. My dad (A. A. Prout) is a pretty famous watercolorist, and it was my greatest honor to watch him paint when I was a child. It showed me how artistry is the energy of creation and how it can also manifest abundance.

You are an artist, whether you realize it or not. Your life is your canvas, and every choice you make adds another stroke to the masterpiece of your existence. The way you arrange your home, the meals you prepare, the words you speak—all of these are expressions of your innate artistry. Embrace the artist within you. See the beauty in the everyday moments and find ways to amplify it. Let your unique style shine through in all that you do. The world needs your particular brand of creativity, your special way of seeing and being. Don't be afraid to express yourself boldly and authentically. Your art has the power to touch hearts, open minds, and heal souls.

DEAR UNIVERSE, I embrace the energy of true artistry, expressing my unique vision through every aspect of my life. May my creativity bring beauty and inspiration to the world.

so be it, so it is.

6

conceptualization

THE NEW THOUGHT WRITER PRENTICE MULFORD, who lived from 1834 to 1891, coined the term "thoughts are things" during the late nineteenth century. Mulford's phrase relates to conceptualization by emphasizing that our mental constructs and ideas are not merely abstract but have the power to shape our reality and influence the world around us.

Your mind is a powerful tool for shaping reality. Before anything can exist in the physical world, it must first be conceived in thought.

DEAR UNIVERSE,
I am a master of conceptualization, effortlessly transforming abstract ideas into tangible realities. Guide my thoughts toward concepts that serve the highest good.

so be it,
so it is.

As you move through your day, practice the art of conceptualization. See the invisible connections between ideas, envision new possibilities, and give form to the formless. Your ability to conceptualize is the first step in bringing your dreams to life. When faced with a challenge, take a step back and reimagine the entire concept. What if you approached it from a completely different angle? What if the problem itself is an opportunity in disguise? By honing your skills of conceptualization, you become a true architect of your own reality.

expression

HOW DO YOU LET YOUR INNER LIGHT SHINE? Expression is the bridge between your inner world and the outer reality. It's through expression that you share your unique gifts with the world. Your voice, your movements, your creations—all of these are channels for your soul to speak. Don't hold back. Let your truth flow freely, whether through words, art, dance, or any other form that calls to you. Your authentic expression has the power to move mountains and touch hearts. Remember, there is only one you in all of time and space. Your perspective, your story, your way of being in the world is precious and irreplaceable. Express yourself fully and watch as the Universe responds in kind.

DEAR UNIVERSE, I am courageously embodying the expression of my authentic self. I allow my inner truth to flow freely into the world. May my unique voice inspire and uplift others.

so be it,
so it is.

muse

HAVE YOU EVER FELT A SUDDEN rush of inspiration, as if touched by an unseen force? That is the muse whispering energy codes to your soul. The muse isn't some external entity—it's the wellspring of creativity that lives within you, always ready to bubble up with fresh ideas and insights. Nurture a relationship with your inner muse. Create space in your life for quiet contemplation and playful exploration.

Pay attention to the subtle nudges and flashes of inspiration that come to you throughout the day. When you honor these gifts from your muse, you open yourself to a constant flow of creative energy. Let your muse guide you toward your highest creative potential. Also remember, you are the muse, you are the creative energy manifesting in each and every moment.

DEAR UNIVERSE,
I am attuned to the whispers of my inner muse, receptive to divine inspiration in all its forms. May creativity flow through me abundantly and joyfully.

*so be it,
so it is.*

invention

WITHIN YOU LIES THE POWER TO bring entirely new things into existence. Invention isn't reserved for scientists and engineers—it's a fundamental human capacity that you can tap into every day.

Look at the world around you with fresh eyes. What needs aren't being met? What processes could be simplified? What beauty is waiting to be born? Your unique combination of experiences, skills, and insights gives you the ability to see solutions that no one else can. Embrace your role as an inventor in your own life.

Experiment, tinker, and don't be afraid to fail. Each attempt brings you closer to that breakthrough invention that could change everything.

DEAR UNIVERSE, I am the embodiment of invention, bringing new ideas and solutions into the world. Guide my creativity toward inventions that serve the highest good of all.

so be it, so it is.

spark

THERE'S A DIVINE SPARK WITHIN YOU, a flame of potential just waiting to be fanned into a roaring fire. This spark is your passion, your purpose, your reason for being. It's what makes your heart sing and your soul soar. Have you been nurturing your inner spark, or has it been neglected, buried under the weight of daily responsibilities?

Today, make a commitment to tend to that sacred flame. What activities make you lose track of time? What causes set your heart ablaze with purpose? Feed your spark with attention and intention. As it grows stronger, it will light the way forward on your path, illuminating opportunities and guiding you toward your highest potential.

DEAR UNIVERSE,
I nurture the divine spark within me, allowing it to grow into a beacon of passion and purpose. May my inner fire inspire and warm those around me.

*so be it,
so it is.*

dream

WHEN WAS THE LAST TIME YOU allowed yourself to dream big? Really big? Your dreams are not mere fantasies—they are glimpses of your potential future, seeds of greatness waiting to be nurtured into reality. All of the things I have manifested into my life, such as dream homes, miracle babies, and creative projects always first began as dreams.

Close your eyes and envision the life you truly desire, free from the constraints of what you believe is possible. What does it look like? Most importantly, how does it feel? Let yourself sink into that vision, absorbing every detail. Your dreams are the blueprint for your destiny. By daring to dream boldly, you set in motion forces beyond your understanding. The Universe conspires to make your dreams a reality when you have the courage to first dream them into being.

DEAR UNIVERSE,
I dream courageously and without limits, knowing that my visions are seeds of future realities. Guide me as I nurture my dreams into manifestation.

so be it,
so it is.

12

ingenuity

YOUR MIND IS A TREASURE TROVE OF INGENUITY, capable of finding creative solutions to any challenge. Ingenuity isn't about having all the answers—it's about approaching problems with flexibility, curiosity, and resourcefulness. The next time you face an obstacle, resist the urge to give up or seek the easy way out. Instead, view it as an opportunity to exercise your ingenuity. What unconventional approaches haven't been tried?

How can you combine existing ideas in new ways? Your ingenious spirit is a powerful force for positive change in your life and in the world. Trust in your ability to figure things out, no matter how complex the problem may seem.

DEAR UNIVERSE,
I am a wellspring of ingenuity, approaching life's challenges with creativity and resourcefulness. May my innovative spirit lead to solutions that benefit all.

so be it,
so it is.

visionary

LIFT YOUR GAZE BEYOND THE HORIZON of what is known and dare to envision a better world. You are a visionary, capable of seeing possibilities that others miss. Your unique perspective allows you to imagine futures that have yet to be born. Don't dismiss your visions as mere daydreams—they are glimpses of potential realities, waiting for someone bold enough to bring them into being. What do you see when you look to the future?

DEAR UNIVERSE,
I embrace my role as a visionary, seeing beyond current limitations to a world of endless possibilities. May my vision inspire positive change and growth.

so be it,
so it is.

What changes do you long to make in the world? Your vision has the power to inspire and guide others toward a brighter tomorrow. Share your vision fearlessly, and watch as it begins to take shape in the world around you.

14

originality

COPYCAT RUBBISH IS EVERYWHERE. In a world that often encourages conformity, your originality is your greatest strength. There has never been, and will never be, another person quite like you. Your unique blend of experiences, perspectives, and talents allows you to approach life in ways no one else can. Embrace your quirks, celebrate your differences, and let your true colors shine.

When you honor your originality, you give others permission to do the same. Your authentic self-expression is a gift to the world, adding a vibrant hue to the tapestry of human experience. Today, challenge yourself to break free from conventions and express your originality in everything you do.

DEAR UNIVERSE,
I celebrate my originality, expressing my authentic self without fear or hesitation. May my unique perspective bring fresh insights and joy to the world.

so be it,
so it is.

alchemy

YOU ARE AN ALCHEMIST OF THE SOUL, capable of transmuting the base metals of your experiences into gold. Alchemy isn't just an ancient pseudoscience—it's a powerful metaphor for personal transformation. Every challenge you face, every setback you encounter, is raw material waiting to be transformed. What if you could turn your fears into courage, your wounds into wisdom, your pain to power, your failures into stepping stones for success? This is the true work of the inner alchemist. It requires patience, persistence, and a willingness to dive deep into the crucible of your own consciousness.

As you practice this inner alchemy, you'll discover that nothing in your life is wasted—everything can be transformed into something precious and meaningful.

DEAR UNIVERSE,
I am a master of alchemy, transforming all experiences into wisdom, strength, and beauty. May my inner work create ripples of positive change in the world around me.

so be it,
so it is.

insight

WITHIN YOU LIES A WELLSPRING OF WISDOM, waiting to be tapped. Insight isn't about accumulating information—it's about seeing clearly, perceiving the truth that lies beneath the surface. In moments of stillness, when you quiet the chatter of your mind, profound insights can emerge.

DEAR UNIVERSE,
I am open to receiving profound insights, trusting in the wisdom that flows through me. May my inner clarity guide me toward choices that serve my highest good.

so be it,
so it is.

Always remember to pay attention to your intuitive hunches, those flashes of understanding that seem to come from nowhere. These are messages from your deeper self, your higher self, offering guidance and clarity. As you invite your capacity for insight, you'll find yourself making decisions with greater confidence and navigating life's complexities with ease. Trust in your innate wisdom and let it light your path forward.

eureka

THE WORD *EUREKA* ORIGINATES FROM ancient Greece and is famously attributed to the Greek mathematician and inventor Archimedes. According to legend, Archimedes exclaimed "Eureka!"—which means "I have found it!" in Greek—oddly enough when he discovered the principle of buoyancy while taking a bath. This moment of sudden insight and realization has since become synonymous with moments of discovery and inspiration.

Remember the joy of discovery, the exhilaration of a breakthrough moment? Think of finding that edge piece in a jigsaw puzzle or when you remember where you left your phone. That "eureka!" feeling is available to you every day, if you approach life with curiosity and openness. Each challenge you face is an opportunity for a breakthrough. Each question you ask can lead to a moment of illumination. Call forth a mindset of discovery in your daily life. Look at familiar things with fresh eyes. Question your assumptions. Explore new perspectives. As you do, you'll find yourself experiencing more and more of those thrilling "aha!" moments that propel you forward on your journey of growth and understanding.

DEAR UNIVERSE,
I am a magnet for breakthrough moments, constantly discovering new insights and solutions. May my journey be filled with joyful revelations that expand my understanding.

so be it,
so it is.

resonance

HAVE YOU EVER FELT A DEEP, inexplicable connection to a piece of music, a work of art, or another person? That's energetic resonance—a powerful force that can align your inner world with the outer one.

Like a tuning fork vibrating in harmony with a specific frequency, you have the ability to resonate with the energies, ideas, and experiences that align with your true self. Pay attention to what resonates with you. These resonant experiences are signposts, guiding you toward your authentic path. When you live in resonance with your deepest values and passions, you create a life that feels profoundly right and deeply satisfying. Make sure you surround yourself with people who feel in alignment with your soul. My favorite thing to do is share many moments of laughter with my beloved, with my children, and with my friends.

Today, seek out experiences that make your soul hum with recognition. As you align more fully with what resonates, you'll find yourself naturally attracting opportunities and relationships that support your highest good.

DEAR UNIVERSE,
I am attuned to the resonance of my true self, creating harmony within and without. May my aligned vibrations inspire and uplift those around me.

so be it,
so it is.

creativity

CREATIVITY IS NOT A TALENT RESERVED for a chosen few—it's a fundamental aspect of being human. You are a creative being, whether you realize it or not. Every time you solve a problem, express an emotion, or imagine a new possibility, you're engaging your creative powers.

Today, challenge yourself to approach life more creatively. How can you add a touch of whimsy or "wow factor" to your daily routine? What new combinations can you create with the resources at hand? As you flex your creative muscles, you'll discover new solutions, experience greater joy, and unlock potential you never knew you had. Let your creativity flow freely and watch as it transforms your world.

DEAR UNIVERSE,
I am an open channel for limitless creativity, bringing fresh ideas and beauty into the world. May my creative spirit flourish and inspire positive change in all areas of my life.

so be it,
so it is.

20

transformation

MY WORK AS A MANIFESTATION TEACHER over the last decade has given me the deepest honor of working with some pretty incredible people to create transformation in their lives. I've seen so many beautiful miracles manifest. One of my clients manifested her soulmate after years of searching. Another client was given an unwelcomed medical diagnosis and was able to go into complete remission. One of my favorite clients quit his job after seven years in a corporate role to pursue his music career and completely upleveled his mindset around work and abundance.

That same potential for radical change exists within you. Transformation isn't just about making small improvements—it's about fundamentally reimagining what's possible. It's about shedding old limitations and emerging as something entirely new. Your life is a canvas, and you have the power to paint a completely different picture at any moment.

DEAR UNIVERSE,
I embrace the power of transformation, constantly evolving into the highest version of myself. May my journey inspire others to embrace positive change.

so be it,
so it is.

What aspects of your life are calling for transformation? What old patterns or beliefs are you ready to release? Embrace the discomfort of change, for it is the cocoon from which your highest self will emerge. Remember, true transformation isn't just about changing what you do—it's about changing who you are at your core.

revelation

LIFE IS FULL OF REVELATIONS WAITING TO UNFOLD, if only we have eyes to see and ears to hear. Each day brings opportunities for new understanding, for sudden clarity that can shift your entire perspective. Stay open to these moments of revelation. They might come in a flash of insight during meditation, while reading this book, or even in a casual conversation with a stranger. They might emerge from a challenge that forces you to see things differently.

Whatever form they take, these revelations are guideposts on your journey of growth and self-discovery. Embrace them, learn from them, and let them guide you toward a deeper understanding of yourself and the world around you.

DEAR UNIVERSE, I am open to receiving divine revelations that expand my consciousness and understanding. May each revelation guide me closer to my highest truth and purpose.

so be it,
so it is.

22

resourcefulness

WITHIN YOU LIES AN INFINITE WELLSPRING of resourcefulness, waiting to be tapped. Resourcefulness isn't about having everything you need—it's about making the most of what you have. It's the ability to see potential where others see limitations, to find creative solutions with the tools at hand. When faced with a challenge, resist the urge to focus on what you lack. Instead, take stock of your available resources—your skills, your knowledge, your connections, and even the seemingly unrelated objects around you.

How can you combine these in new ways to overcome obstacles? As you call in your resourcefulness, you'll find that you already have everything you need to thrive and succeed.

DEAR UNIVERSE,
I have infinite access to resourcefulness. I creatively use all available tools to overcome any challenge. May my ingenuity and adaptability lead me to innovative solutions.

so be it,
so it is.

emergence

HAVE YOU EVER WATCHED A SEEDLING push through the soil, defying gravity to reach for the sun? At the time I am writing this, I've been planting seeds in flowerpots with my daughters. When we planted the seeds, we meditated and asked the Universe to help with the accelerated growth of the seeds. Within just forty-eight hours, the new growth had sprouted. It was truly a miracle to witness how speedy the growth was.

That same force of emergence exists within you, constantly urging you to grow beyond your current limits. Emergence is the process of becoming, of allowing your true nature to unfold in its own time and way. It's not about forcing or striving, but about creating the right conditions for your innate potential to naturally express itself. What parts of you are ready to emerge? What dormant talents or long-held dreams are stirring just beneath the surface? Trust in the wisdom of your own unfolding. Like a flower blooming, your emergence cannot be rushed, only nurtured. Provide yourself with the nourishment, space, and patience you need to fully become who you are meant to be.

DEAR UNIVERSE,
I trust in the natural process of my own emergence, allowing my true self to unfold in divine timing. May my growth inspire others to embrace their own becoming.

so be it,
so it is.

essence

WHAT IS THE CORE OF WHO YOU ARE, beneath all the layers of conditioning and expectation? Your essence is your fundamental nature, the purest expression of your being. It's what remains when all else is stripped away. In a world that often encourages us to conform, connecting with your essence is a radical act of self-discovery and authenticity. Take a moment to peel back the layers of shoulds and supposed-tos.

DEAR UNIVERSE, I honor and express my true essence, allowing my authentic self to shine brightly in all that I do. May my genuine presence inspire others to embrace their own unique nature.

so be it, so it is.

What qualities shine through consistently, no matter the circumstance? What values do you hold dear, even when they're challenged? Your essence isn't something you need to create or achieve—it's already there, waiting to be recognized and expressed. As you align more fully with your essence, you'll find a deep sense of peace and purpose. You'll move through the world with grace and power, because you're no longer fighting against your true nature.

genius

THERE'S A UNIQUE GENIUS WITHIN YOU, waiting to be expressed. This isn't about having a high IQ or being a prodigy—it's about recognizing and cultivating your innate gifts. Your genius might lie in your ability to connect with others, your knack for solving puzzles, your love for playing trivia games with your best friend, or your talent for bringing beauty into the world. It's the thing you do that feels effortless, that puts you in a state of flow. Don't compare your genius to others or dismiss it because it seems ordinary to you. The world needs your particular brand of brilliance. Today, commit to exploring and expressing your genius. As you do, you'll find yourself stepping into your full power and making your unique contribution to the world.

DEAR UNIVERSE,
I embrace and express my unique genius, sharing my gifts freely with the world. May my innate talents flourish and bring light to others.

so be it,
so it is.

26

intuition

LISTEN CLOSELY. CAN YOU HEAR THE whisper of your intuition? It's always there, guiding you toward your highest good, if only you learn to tune in. Your intuition is your inner compass, a deep knowing that goes beyond logic and reason. It speaks to you through gut feelings, sudden insights, and sometimes even through your dreams. In a world that often values rational thinking above all else, it takes courage to trust your intuition. But when you do, you tap into a wellspring of wisdom that can guide you unerringly through life's complexities.

Today, practice listening to your intuition. What is it telling you about your current path?

DEAR UNIVERSE,
I trust and follow my intuition, allowing its wisdom to guide me toward my highest good. May my inner knowing lead me to choices that align with my true path.

so be it,
so it is.

illumination

IN THE DARKEST NIGHT, a single candle can illuminate an entire room. You are that candle, capable of bringing light to the shadows, both within yourself and in the world around you. Illumination comes in many forms—it might be a moment of clarity that dispels confusion, a flash of insight that solves a long-standing problem, or an act of kindness that brightens someone's day. As you move through your life, consciously seek to be a source of illumination.

Share your knowledge, spread positivity, shine the light of awareness on issues that matter. Remember, the brighter you shine, the more you inspire others to do the same.

DEAR UNIVERSE,
I am a beacon of illumination, spreading light and clarity wherever I go. May my presence dispel darkness and inspire others to shine their own light.

so be it,
so it is.

28

aspiration

WHAT DO YOU ASPIRE TO? Your aspirations are the North Star that guides your journey, pulling you forward toward your highest potential. They're more than just goals—they're a vision of who you can become, of the impact you can make on the world.

DEAR UNIVERSE, my aspirations lift me higher, guiding me toward my greatest potential and most meaningful contributions. May my journey inspire others to reach for their dreams.

so be it, so it is.

Take a moment to connect with your deepest aspirations. What kind of person do you want to be? What mark do you want to leave on the world?

Let these aspirations inform your daily choices and actions. As you align your life with your highest aspirations, you'll find yourself living with greater purpose and fulfillment.

wonder

I WAS FORTY-FOUR YEARS OLD THE first time I saw fireflies. It was a wonder to behold—these magical tiny lights lighting up randomly in my garden. I felt like a little kid seeing the lights of a newly decorated Christmas tree being plugged into the wall socket.

When was the last time you felt a sense of wonder? That childlike awe at the beauty and mystery of the world? Wonder is the doorway to joy, creativity, and spiritual growth. It opens your eyes to the magic that surrounds you every day. In a world that can sometimes feel jaded and cynical, cultivating a sense of wonder is a radical act. It's a choice to see the extraordinary in the ordinary, to approach life with openness and curiosity. Today, challenge yourself to rediscover wonder. Look at familiar things with fresh eyes. Ask questions. Allow yourself to be amazed by the miracle of existence.

DEAR UNIVERSE,
I embrace life with a sense of wonder, marveling at the beauty and mystery that surround me. May my open heart and curious mind lead me to joyful discoveries.

so be it,
so it is.

30

devotion

WHAT ARE YOU DEVOTED TO? WHO are you devoted to? Devotion is the heartbeat of a purposeful life. It's the unwavering commitment to something greater than yourself—a cause, a craft, a relationship, or a spiritual path. When you live with devotion, you infuse every action with meaning and intentionality. You persevere through challenges because you're connected to a deeper purpose. Devotion doesn't mean you never have doubts or struggles. Rather, it's the choice to recommit every day, to show up fully even when it's difficult. Reflect on what truly matters to you. How can you bring a sense of devotion to your daily life?

DEAR UNIVERSE,
I live with unwavering devotion to my highest purpose, infusing each day with meaning and intentionality. May my dedication inspire others to live with passion and commitment.

so be it,
so it is.

MONTH 10

courage and
fearlessness

In each moment, you have the inflection point to choose either fear or love. However, you can't spiritually bypass the opportunity to grow, and facing fears is a key component of personal growth. This month, we focus on building courage and embracing a fearless attitude to help you through different chapters of transformation in your life.

Empowering yourself to step out of your comfort zone and take (safe) risks is crucial for manifesting your dreams. By fostering fearlessness, you open up to new opportunities and experiences.

REMEMBER: Courage is your magical portal to new horizons. Embrace bravery, conquer your fears, and see how your boldness propels you toward your aspirations.

bravery

IN FEBRUARY OF 2024, I was placed on a stretcher and terrified for my life as the doors of the ambulance slammed shut. My heart rate was dangerously elevated because of the private stress and pain within my marriage. I was either having a panic attack or a heart attack (which I wasn't, thankfully), and I had to summon the bravery to navigate the present moment of distress.

Bravery isn't the absence of fear, but the decision to move forward despite it. No matter what your story is, you possess an inner strength that's waiting to be unleashed. It's in the way you face each day or moments of distress. It's in the small acts of courage that often go unnoticed. Remember, every hero's journey begins with a single, brave choice. Your path may be uncertain, but your spirit is unbreakable. Embrace the challenges that come your way, for they are the chisel that shapes your character. In moments of doubt, stand tall and remind yourself of the battles you've already won. You are the author of your story, and bravery is your pen. Write a tale that inspires, a narrative of resilience and triumph. The world needs your unique brand of courage—the kind that whispers "yes" when everything else screams "no." So step into the arena of life with your head held high, knowing that bravery isn't just about grand gestures, but about the quiet determination to keep going, one brave heartbeat at a time.

DEAR UNIVERSE, grant me the courage to face my fears, the strength to overcome obstacles, and the wisdom to recognize my own bravery in everyday acts.

so be it, so it is.

courage

YOU ARE A WELLSPRING OF UNTAPPED COURAGE. Each day presents new opportunities to showcase your inner strength, to rise above the challenges that life throws your way. Courage isn't just about grand gestures or heroic deeds; it's in the small choices you make every day. It's in the voice that speaks up for what's right, even when it quivers. It's in the hand that reaches out to help, even when it trembles. Your courage is a flame that burns bright within you, illuminating the path forward even in the darkest of times. Embrace this power within you, nurture it, and watch as it transforms not just your life, but the lives of those around you. Remember, courage is contagious. Your act of bravery today could inspire countless others tomorrow. So stand tall, face your fears, and let your courageous spirit soar. The world is waiting for you to show up in all your bold, beautiful glory.

DEAR UNIVERSE, empower me with unwavering courage to face life's challenges and inspire others through my actions. Let my bravery light the way.

so be it,
so it is.

3

fearlessness

FEAR HAS DEFINITELY BEEN AN ELEMENT of motivation in my life. I've been scared of some pretty interesting things, such as public speaking or singing in front of others. Then I asked myself the question: "What would you do if fear no longer held you back?"

Imagine the possibilities that would unfold if you embraced a fearless mindset. Fearlessness isn't about the absence of fear, but about moving forward despite it. It's about recognizing that on the other side of your comfort zone resides growth, opportunity, and a life fully lived. You have the power to stare down your doubts and uncertainties, to push past the boundaries that have held you captive. Every time you choose inspired action over hesitation, you're flexing your fearless muscles. Remember, the most extraordinary achievements in history were accomplished by ordinary people who decided to be fearless. Your journey to fearlessness starts with a single step. Take it. Embrace the unknown, for it holds the key to your greatest adventures. Let your fearless spirit guide you to new heights, new experiences, and a life rich with purpose and passion.

DEAR UNIVERSE, instill in me the spirit of fearlessness to embrace life's challenges and opportunities with open arms and an adventurous heart.

so be it,
so it is.

daring

I ALWAYS ASK MY PRIVATE MENTORING clients to dare to dream bigger than they ever have before. Being daring is a powerful energy when it comes to manifestation. Your aspirations are the seeds of your future reality, and it's time to plant them with audacious hope. Being daring isn't just about taking risks; it's about believing in your own potential and abilities to create change, to innovate, to leave your mark on the world. It's about stepping out of the shadows of self-doubt and into the spotlight of your own making. Every great achievement started as a daring idea in someone's mind. You have those ideas within you too. Nurture them, give them a voice, and watch as they transform from mere thoughts into tangible realities. Your daring spirit is the key that unlocks doors to opportunities you've never imagined. Go ahead, take that leap of faith.

Propose that wild idea. Start that project you've been putting off. The world is waiting for your unique brand of daring.

DEAR UNIVERSE, grant me the daring energy to dream big, the courage to act on those dreams, and the resilience to persevere in the face of challenges.

so be it,
so it is.

5

audacious

AUDACITY IS THE SPARK THAT IGNITES REVOLUTIONS, both personal and global. It's the force that drives you to challenge the status quo, to question the boundaries of what's possible. Your audacious spirit is a gift to the world, a beacon of inspiration for those who have forgotten how to dream big. Embrace your boldness, your willingness to stand out and speak up.

In a world that often encourages conformity, your audacity is a refreshing burst of color. It's the courage to be authentically you, unapologetically and wholeheartedly. Remember, every great innovation, every paradigm shift, started with an audacious idea. Your audacity today could be the catalyst for a better tomorrow. It could also be your legacy. Let your imagination run wild, let your voice rise above the noise, and let your actions reflect the magnitude of your dreams. The world needs your audacious spirit now more than ever.

DEAR UNIVERSE, fuel my audacious spirit with the confidence to challenge norms, inspire change, and leave a lasting impact on the world.

so be it, so it is.

valor

VALOR ISN'T RESERVED FOR BATTLEFIELDS or moments of crisis; it resides within you as unconditional love, waiting to be called upon in everyday acts of courage. It's the strength that propels you forward when the path ahead seems daunting. Your valor is evident in the way you face life's challenges head-on, in your willingness to stand up for what's right, with love, even when it's difficult.

It's in the compassion you show to others, and the resilience you demonstrate in the face of adversity. Remember, valor isn't about being fearless; it's about acknowledging your fears and moving forward anyway. It's about choosing integrity over comfort, truth over convenience. Your valor has the power to inspire others, to create ripples of courage that extend far beyond your immediate circle. Embrace your inner hero, for in doing so, you give others permission to do the same. Let your valor shine bright, illuminating the path for those who may be lost in darkness and send them love in your heart and mind.

DEAR UNIVERSE, ignite the flame of valor and unconditional love within me, guiding my actions with courage, integrity, and unwavering commitment to what's right.

so be it, so it is.

boldness

YOUR BOLDNESS IS THE KEY THAT unlocks doors to extraordinary possibilities. It's the voice that speaks up when others remain silent, the step you take when others hesitate. Boldness isn't about being loud or aggressive; it's about being unapologetically authentic and true to your convictions. For instance, my mother, Louise (to whom this book is dedicated), has the most emphatic energy when she is practicing boldness. As her daughter, this taught me to have the courage to stand out, to be different, to challenge the norm.

Your bold spirit has the power to inspire change, to motivate others, to leave an indelible mark on the world. Embrace your uniqueness, your ideas, your dreams—no matter how unconventional they may seem. Remember, history is shaped by those bold enough to envision a different future and brave enough to work toward it.

DEAR UNIVERSE, may my spirit allow me to speak my truth, pursue my dreams with boldness, and inspire others through my authentic self-expression.

so be it, so it is.

heroic

THE HERO'S JOURNEY ISN'T JUST a tale in books or movies; it's the story of your life. Every day, you have the opportunity to be the hero in your own narrative and in the lives of those around you. Heroism isn't about grand gestures or superhuman feats; it's about the small acts of kindness, the moments of perseverance in the face of adversity, the choice to do what's right even when it's hard and especially when no one is looking. Your heroic spirit is evident in the way you face your challenges, in how you lift others up, in your resilience when life knocks you down.

Remember, heroes aren't born; they're made through the choices they make every day. You have the power to be a force for good, to make a positive impact, to change someone's world. Embrace your inner hero, for in doing so, you inspire others to find the hero within themselves. Let your actions speak of courage, your words of compassion, and your presence of strength.

DEAR UNIVERSE, awaken heroic energy within me, guiding my actions with courage, compassion, and the power to make a positive difference in the world.

so be it,
so it is.

indomitable

YOUR INDOMITABLE SPIRIT IS AN UNSHAKABLE foundation upon which you can build your dreams. It's the unwavering determination that keeps you moving forward, even when the path is unclear or obstacles seem insurmountable. Being indomitable doesn't mean you never doubt or falter; it means you choose to persevere despite those moments of uncertainty. It's the inner strength that whispers "keep going" when everything else screams "give up." Your indomitable nature is a beacon of hope, not just for yourself, but for those around you who draw inspiration from your steadfast commitment.

DEAR UNIVERSE, fortify my indomitable spirit, granting me the strength to persevere through challenges and the determination to achieve my goals.

so be it, so it is.

Your determination today is paving the way for your success tomorrow. Try to stand firm in your convictions, hold fast to your goals, and let your indomitable spirit guide you through life's storms.

gutsy

YOUR GUTSY NATURE IS THE SPARK that ignites extraordinary adventures and breakthrough moments. It's that flutter in your stomach when you're about to take a leap of faith, that rush of adrenaline when you're pushing your boundaries. Being gutsy isn't about being reckless or mindless; it's about having the courage to follow your instincts, to take calculated risks, to step out of your comfort zone in pursuit of growth and fulfillment. Your gutsiness is what sets you apart, what allows you to seize opportunities that others might let slip by. It's the force that propels you to speak up, stand out, and make your mark on the world.

Remember, every innovative idea, every revolutionary change, started with someone gutsy enough to challenge the status quo. Embrace your audacious spirit, for it is the key to unlocking your full potential. Let your gutsy nature guide you to new experiences, new connections, and new heights of achievement.

DEAR UNIVERSE, fuel my gutsy spirit with the courage to take risks, embrace new challenges, and boldly pursue my dreams without hesitation.

so be it,
so it is.

tenacious

YOUR TENACITY IS THE UNBREAKABLE THREAD that weaves your dreams into reality. It's the grit that keeps you going when the going gets tough, the perseverance that turns obstacles into stepping stones. Being tenacious means holding on to your goals with an iron grip, refusing to let setbacks or failures deter you from your path. It's about getting up one more time than you fall, about seeing challenges as opportunities for growth rather than roadblocks. Your tenacious spirit is a force to be reckoned with—it's what transforms ordinary individuals into extraordinary achievers.

Remember, success isn't about never failing; it's about never giving up. Your tenacity today is laying the foundation for your triumphs tomorrow.

Try if you will to dig deep, hold fast to your aspirations, and let your tenacious nature drive you forward.

DEAR UNIVERSE, infuse me with the unwavering energy of tenacity to pursue my goals, overcome obstacles, and turn my dreams into reality through persistent effort.

*so be it,
so it is.*

dauntless

WHEN MY MANIFESTATION MENTORING CLIENT Jane lost her job, instead of succumbing to despair, she saw it as an opportunity to pursue her long-held dream of starting her own business. With a dauntless spirit, she embraced the uncertainty, poured her savings into her passion project, and within a year, her small startup had grown into a thriving company that employed dozens of people in her community. A dauntless spirit knows no bounds. It's the fearless energy that propels you to face challenges head-on, to dive into the unknown with open arms. Being dauntless doesn't mean you never feel fear; it means you don't let fear dictate your actions. It's about embracing life's adventures with enthusiasm, about seeing opportunities where others see obstacles.

DEAR UNIVERSE, ignite my dauntless spirit, granting me the courage to face fears, embrace challenges, and live boldly without hesitation.

so be it,
so it is.

Your dauntless nature is a beacon of inspiration, encouraging others to step out of their comfort zones and into the realm of possibility. It's the force that drives innovation, sparks change, and pushes the boundaries of what's possible.

13

determined

YOUR DETERMINATION IS THE ENGINE THAT drives your dreams forward. It's the unwavering focus that keeps you on track, the persistent effort that turns goals into achievements. Being determined means setting your sights on a target and refusing to let anything deter you from reaching it. It's about maintaining your resolve even when the path is difficult, about finding alternative routes when obstacles block your way.

> **DEAR UNIVERSE,** strengthen my determined spirit to pursue my goals relentlessly, overcome challenges, and turn my aspirations into tangible achievements.
>
> *so be it, so it is.*

Your determined spirit is a powerful force—it's what separates those who dream from those who do. Remember, success is often not about having the best resources, but about making the best use of what you have through sheer determination.

Your determined efforts today are laying the groundwork for your future successes. So stay focused, keep pushing forward, and let your determination be the driving force in your life.

intrepid

I HAD A "PINCH MYSELF" MOMENT eating dinner on a luxury yacht as we were about to anchor in Monte Carlo, Monaco. Never in a million years did I ever think that I would be sailing across the Mediterranean Sea with a group of world-famous authors, entrepreneurs, and poker players. I was wearing a black cocktail dress and heels, about to go and explore this glamorous district. When I was first invited, I declined the offer, and then my intrepid spirit answered the call. Magic happens when you say yes to new and exciting adventures.

Your intrepid spirit is the compass that guides you through uncharted territories. It's the courage that propels you to explore new ideas, to venture beyond the familiar, to challenge the boundaries of what's possible. Being intrepid isn't about being fearless; it's about acknowledging your fears and moving forward anyway. It's about embracing the unknown with curiosity rather than trepidation. Your intrepid nature is what allows you to grow, to innovate, to discover new facets of yourself and the world around you. It's the force that has driven explorers, inventors, and visionaries throughout history. Remember, every great discovery, every paradigm shift, started with someone intrepid enough to question the status quo. Always let your adventurous spirit lead the way, let it push you out of your comfort zone and into the realm of endless possibilities, and who knows, you might end up in Monte Carlo!

DEAR UNIVERSE, kindle my intrepid spirit, giving me the courage to explore new horizons, embrace the unknown, and live life adventurously.

so be it, so it is.

15

spirited

YOUR SPIRITED NATURE IS THE VIBRANT energy that colors your world with passion and enthusiasm. It's the zest for life that makes every day an adventure, every challenge an opportunity. Being spirited means approaching life with a positive attitude, with an eagerness to experience all it has to offer. It's about infusing your actions with energy, your words with warmth, your relationships with genuine connection. Your spirited approach to life is contagious—it uplifts those around you, inspiring them to embrace their own passions and live more fully. Remember, a spirited life is not one without hardships, but one where challenges are met with resilience and optimism. Your spirited nature today is creating a ripple effect of positivity that extends far beyond your immediate circle. It's the essence that makes you unique. Try to let your enthusiasm shine bright, let your passion fuel your pursuits, and let your spirited energy be a force for good in the world.

DEAR UNIVERSE,
ignite my spirited nature, filling me with enthusiasm, passion, and joy to approach each day with vibrant energy and positivity.

so be it,
so it is.

unshakable

YOUR UNSHAKABLE SPIRIT IS THE BEDROCK upon which you build your life. It's the inner strength that keeps you steady in the face of life's storms, the unwavering conviction that anchors you to your values and goals. Being unshakable doesn't mean you never face doubt or difficulty; it means you have the resilience to withstand challenges without losing your core. It's about maintaining your integrity, your purpose, your hope, even when the world around you is in chaos. Your unshakable nature is a source of stability not just for yourself, but for those around you who draw strength from your steadfast presence.

Remember, the most influential people in history were those who remained unshakable in their beliefs and their pursuit of what's right. Your unshakable spirit today is laying the foundation for a future built on strength and principle. So stand firm in your convictions, hold fast to your values, and let your unshakable nature be a beacon of stability in an ever-changing world.

DEAR UNIVERSE, fortify my unshakable spirit, granting me the strength to stand firm in my convictions and remain steadfast in the face of life's challenges.

so be it, so it is.

17

adventurous

WHAT HAVEN'T YOU TRIED? Is there a part of you yearning to break free from the mundane? Your adventurous spirit is the key to unlocking a life full of rich experiences and personal growth. It's not about grand expeditions or daredevil stunts; it's about approaching each day with a sense of curiosity and openness. Being adventurous means saying "yes" to new opportunities, stepping out of your comfort zone, and embracing the unknown. It's in trying that new hobby, striking up a conversation with a stranger, or taking a different route home. It could even be about trying a new food or learning to mix up a new cocktail. Your adventurous nature has the power to transform the ordinary into the extraordinary, to turn everyday moments into memorable experiences. Remember, life's greatest adventures often begin with a single step into the unfamiliar. Always let your adventurous spirit guide you. Seek out new experiences, challenge yourself, and approach life with a sense of wonder. The world is vast and full of possibilities, waiting for your adventurous soul to explore.

DEAR UNIVERSE, ignite my adventurous spirit, guiding me to embrace new experiences, take bold risks, and live life to its fullest potential.

so be it, so it is.

stalwart

YOUR STALWART NATURE IS THE UNWAVERING force that keeps you standing tall in the face of adversity. It's the inner strength that allows you to remain true to your principles, even when it's difficult or unpopular. Being stalwart means being a pillar of reliability and consistency, someone others can depend on in times of need. It's about staying committed to your goals, your values, and your loved ones, no matter what challenges arise. Your stalwart spirit is a beacon of hope and stability in an often chaotic world. It's the quality that turns ordinary individuals into leaders and role models. Remember, history is shaped by those who had the stalwart courage to stand up for what's right, even in the face of opposition. People like Rosa Parks, for instance, are truly inspirational. Despite facing harassment, death threats, and economic hardship after her arrest, Parks never wavered in her stance against racial discrimination. Her stalwart nature was evident in her ability to stand firm in her convictions, even in the face of a system designed to intimidate and oppress.

Your unwavering commitment today is creating a better tomorrow. So, if you can, stand firm in your convictions, be a rock for those around you, and let your stalwart nature shine through in all you do.

DEAR UNIVERSE, strengthen my stalwart spirit, empowering me to stand firm in my principles and be a pillar of strength for myself and others.

so be it,
so it is.

valiant

YOUR VALIANT SPIRIT IS A RADIANT flame that burns within, fueled by the pure energy of your soul. It's the embodiment of courage, noble purpose, and boundless love. This inner light drives you to stand up for what's right, to protect the vulnerable, and to face challenges with unwavering determination and compassion. Being valiant isn't about seeking external glory or recognition; it's about honoring the divine spark within you and expressing it through acts of love and courage.

DEAR UNIVERSE, ignite my valiant spirit, giving me the courage to stand up for what's right and the strength to face challenges with unwavering determination and with the awareness for the greatest good and love for all.

so be it,
so it is.

Your valiance springs from a deep well of self-love and universal connection. It's the courage to speak truth with kindness, to defend your principles with grace, and to take action with a heart full of empathy when others hesitate. This inner strength allows you to stand firm in your convictions while remaining open and loving toward all.

nerve

WHEN WAS THE LAST TIME YOU felt that exhilarating rush of pushing your boundaries? Your nerve is that spark of daring that propels you beyond your comfort zone. It's not recklessness, but rather a calculated boldness that allows you to seize opportunities others might miss. Having nerve means trusting your instincts, taking calculated risks, and believing in your ability to handle the outcome. It's about having the guts to speak up, to stand out, to be the first to try something new. Your nerve is what turns dreams into reality, ideas into innovations. It's the quality that entrepreneurs, leaders, and changemakers all tend to share. If you can, summon your nerve. Take that leap of faith. Propose that daring idea.

DEAR UNIVERSE, bolster my nerve, granting me the audacity to take calculated risks, seize opportunities, and boldly pursue my aspirations.

so be it, so it is.

steadfast

YOUR STEADFAST NATURE IS THE ANCHOR that keeps you grounded in a world of constant change. It's the unwavering commitment to your values, your goals, and your loved ones that defines your character. Being steadfast doesn't mean being inflexible; rather, it's about maintaining your core principles while adapting to life's challenges. It's the perseverance that keeps you moving forward, even when the path is difficult or unclear. Your steadfast spirit is a source of stability and inspiration for those around you. It's the quality that turns promises into actions, dreams into achievements. Remember, the most enduring legacies are built by those who remained steadfast in their pursuit of what truly matters. For example, Martha Stewart's career spans over five decades, beginning in the 1970s when she started a small catering business that grew into a lifestyle empire. Through her iconic books, television shows, and *Martha Stewart Living* magazine, she has influenced generations, withstanding challenges like a five-month prison sentence in 2004, from which she rebounded stronger, continuing to build her brand and legacy well into her eighties.

DEAR UNIVERSE, reinforce my steadfast spirit, empowering me to remain true to my values and persist in my goals with unwavering dedication.

so be it, so it is.

Your consistent efforts today are laying the foundation for a lifetime of integrity and accomplishment. So hold fast to your convictions. Be the reliable friend, the dedicated worker, the committed partner. Let your steadfast nature be the bedrock upon which you build a life of purpose and meaning.

unflinching

HAVE YOU EVER HAD A STARING contest with someone? You might have the best of intentions not to blink and understand that if you flinch, you lose. Your unflinching spirit works the same way. The steely resolve that keeps you moving forward, even in the face of adversity. It's the inner strength that allows you to look challenges straight in the eye without backing down (or blinking). Being unflinching doesn't mean you're fearless; it means you have the courage to face your fears head-on.

It's about maintaining your composure under pressure, standing firm in your convictions, and refusing to compromise your integrity. Your unflinching nature is what turns obstacles into opportunities, setbacks into comebacks. Your unwavering determination today is paving the way for a better tomorrow. Always stand tall in the face of challenges. Meet adversity with a steady gaze. Let your unflinching spirit be the force that propels you through life's storms and toward your goals.

DEAR UNIVERSE, fortify my unflinching spirit, granting me the strength to face challenges head-on and the resolve to stand firm in my convictions.

so be it, so it is.

23

lionhearted

YOUR LIONHEARTED NATURE IS THE EMBODIMENT of courage, strength, and nobility. It's the fierce determination that drives you to protect what you love from within, to stand up for what you believe in, and to lead with compassion and integrity. Being lionhearted means facing life's challenges with both strength and grace. It's about having the courage to roar against injustice, the strength to defend the vulnerable, and the wisdom to know when to show mercy. Nelson Mandela's lionhearted nature was evident in his ability to combine strength and courage with compassion and wisdom, making him a powerful force for positive change in the world.

DEAR UNIVERSE,
awaken my lionhearted spirit, filling me with courage to lead, strength to protect, and compassion to inspire positive change.

so be it,
so it is.

Your lionhearted spirit has the power to inspire others, to rally them around a noble cause, to create transformation in the world. Remember, the greatest leaders in history were those who led with a lionheart—courageous in action, steadfast in principle, and compassionate in spirit. Your lionhearted actions today are sowing the seeds of a more just and compassionate world.

unafraid

WHAT WOULD YOU DO IF YOU were completely unafraid? Your unafraid spirit is the key to unlocking your full potential. When I left my second marriage at forty-four, I stepped into the unknown, choosing growth over comfort. That unafraid spirit—the willingness to rebuild and redefine my life from the ground up—revealed a strength I hadn't fully realized. If you were completely unafraid, what bold steps would you take toward becoming the person you're meant to be? Embracing uncertainty and facing fear head-on can unlock a life beyond anything you've imagined, filled with purpose and potential.

Being unafraid means embracing uncertainty as an opportunity for growth, seeing challenges as chances to prove your mettle. It's about trusting in your ability to handle whatever life throws your way. Your unafraid nature has the power to inspire others, to show them what's possible when you refuse to let fear hold you back.

Your fearless actions today are paving the way for a future filled with possibilities. Step out of your comfort zone. Take that leap of faith. Speak your truth. Let your unafraid spirit be the guiding force that propels you toward your dreams and aspirations.

DEAR UNIVERSE, embolden my unafraid spirit, giving me the courage to face my fears, embrace uncertainty, and pursue my dreams without hesitation.

so be it,
so it is.

25

confident

I VIVIDLY REMEMBER WATCHING JUSTIN GUARINI, the runner-up on the first season of *American Idol*, back in 2002. I never could have imagined that years later, he would be the one introducing me as the main keynote speaker at an event in New York City. I had always admired the confidence of people on TV shows and I had assumed that being shy and timid was my fate forevermore. Then, I embodied the energy I needed to speak to many people at once. With practice my confidence grew over time.

Your confidence is the radiant energy that illuminates your path to success. It's not about arrogance or bravado, but a deep-seated belief in your own abilities and worth. Being confident means trusting in your skills, your judgment, and your capacity to learn and grow. It's about carrying yourself with assurance, speaking your mind with conviction, and pursuing your goals with unwavering self-belief. Your confident spirit has the power to open doors, to turn challenges into opportunities, to inspire others to believe in themselves too. Remember, confidence is not about knowing you'll succeed at everything, but believing you can handle whatever comes your way. Your self-assured actions today are laying the groundwork for future achievements. So, stand tall, speak up, and let your light shine.

DEAR UNIVERSE, amplify my confident spirit, granting me unwavering self-belief, inner strength, and the assurance to pursue my goals with conviction.

so be it,
so it is.

unyielding

YOUR UNYIELDING SPIRIT IS THE IMMOVABLE force that keeps you standing strong in the face of life's storms. It's the unwavering determination that refuses to back down from challenges or compromise your values. Being unyielding doesn't mean being rigid or inflexible; it means having the strength to hold firm to your principles and goals, even when the path becomes difficult. It's about persisting in the face of adversity, refusing to give up on your dreams, and standing your ground when it matters most.

Your unyielding nature has the power to move mountains, to overcome seemingly insurmountable obstacles, to achieve what others deem impossible. Your steadfast commitment today is creating a better tomorrow. Persist in your endeavors. Let your unyielding spirit be the bedrock upon which you build your life and legacy.

DEAR UNIVERSE, fortify my unyielding spirit, empowering me to stand firm in my convictions and persist in my goals with unwavering determination.

*so be it,
so it is.*

27

unwavering

YOUR UNWAVERING SPIRIT IS THE STEADY flame that burns bright, even in the darkest of times. It's the consistent dedication to your values, your goals, and your loved ones that defines your character. Being unwavering means staying true to your course, regardless of the obstacles or distractions that may arise. It's about maintaining your focus and commitment, even when the path ahead seems unclear or challenging. Your unwavering nature is a beacon of reliability and strength for those around you. It's the quality that turns dreams into reality, promises into actions. Remember, the most enduring legacies are built by those who remained unwavering in their pursuit of what truly matters.

DEAR UNIVERSE, strengthen my unwavering spirit, granting me the resolve to stay true to my path and the dedication to persist in my goals with steadfast commitment.

so be it, so it is.

Your steady efforts today are creating a foundation for a lifetime of integrity and achievement. Be the dependable friend, the devoted partner, the dedicated professional. Let your unwavering spirit be the guiding light that leads you through life's journey.

persistent

YOUR PERSISTENT NATURE IS THE UNSTOPPABLE force that turns obstacles into stepping stones. It's the relentless drive that keeps you moving forward, even when the path is steep and the progress is slow. Being persistent doesn't mean never failing; it means never giving up. It's about getting back up every time you fall, learning from each setback, and continuing to push toward your goals.

Your persistent spirit has the power to overcome seemingly insurmountable challenges, to achieve what others deem impossible. It's the quality that separates dreamers from achievers, that turns potential into success. Before achieving success with her classic *Little Women*, Louisa May Alcott was advised by publishers to stick to teaching instead of writing.

Remember, every great creative project in history was achieved through persistence in the face of adversity. Your persistent efforts today are laying the groundwork for your future triumphs. Stay committed to your goals. Let your persistent nature be the driving force that propels you toward your dreams and aspirations.

DEAR UNIVERSE, fuel my persistent spirit, giving me the strength to persevere through challenges and the determination to never give up on my goals.

so be it, so it is.

29

bold

YOUR BOLD SPIRIT IS THE VIBRANT energy that colors outside the lines of convention. It's the courage to be uniquely you, to speak your truth, to pursue your dreams without apology. Being bold doesn't mean being reckless; it means having the confidence to take calculated risks, to stand out from the crowd, to challenge the status quo. It's about embracing your authentic self and letting it shine brightly for all to see. Your bold nature has the power to inspire others, to spark change, to leave an indelible mark on the world. It's the quality that innovators, leaders, and trailblazers all possess.

Your audacious actions today are paving the way for a more vibrant, dynamic future. Take that leap of faith. Let your bold spirit be the force that drives you to make a difference in your life and in the lives of others.

DEAR UNIVERSE, ignite my bold spirit, empowering me to embrace my authentic self, take courageous actions, and make a positive impact on the world.

*so be it,
so it is.*

fearless spirit

YOUR FEARLESS SPIRIT IS THE WIND beneath your wings, propelling you to soar beyond the boundaries of the ordinary. It's not the absence of fear, but the courage to spread your wings despite it. Being fearless means embracing life's adventures with open arms, seeing challenges as opportunities for growth rather than obstacles to avoid. It's about trusting in your ability to navigate the unknown, to learn from failures, to rise stronger from every fall. Your fearless nature has the power to inspire others, to show them what's possible when you refuse to let fear dictate your choices.

Your courageous actions today are creating ripples of inspiration that extend far beyond your immediate circle. Always dare to dream big. Take that leap of faith. Embrace the unknown. Let your fearless spirit be the guiding force that leads you to new heights and experiences.

DEAR UNIVERSE, kindle my fearless spirit, granting me the courage to embrace life's adventures and the strength to overcome my fears in pursuit of my dreams.

so be it, so it is.

31

resolute

REFLECT ON THE POWER OF YOUR resolute spirit. It's the unwavering determination that has brought you this far and will carry you forward. Being resolute means having a fixed purpose, a clear direction, and the strength to stay the course, no matter what challenges arise. It's about making decisions with conviction and following through with unwavering commitment. Your resolute nature is the compass that keeps you true to your values and goals, even when the path becomes difficult or unclear. It's the quality that turns intentions into actions, dreams into reality.

DEAR UNIVERSE,
I am resolute in my purpose, steadfast in my actions, and unwavering in my commitment to turning my dreams into reality.

so be it,
so it is.

Remember, the most significant changes in the world were brought about by individuals resolute in their vision and steadfast in their efforts. People like Rosa Parks, Nelson Mandela, Marie Curie, and Frida Kahlo. Your determined actions today are shaping a better tomorrow. Stay true to your purpose. Let your resolute spirit be the driving force that propels you toward your highest aspirations.

MONTH 11

balance and harmony

Creating a balanced life is essential for overall well-being. There's something really magical that happens in your heart when you tune in to the soothing nature of balance. This month, we emphasize the importance of harmony in both personal and professional realms.

Achieving balance ensures that all aspects of your life contribute to your success and happiness. By fostering harmony, you create a supportive environment for growth and fulfillment.

REMEMBER: Striking balance (as best you can) is the key to a harmonious life. Strive for equilibrium, nurture all areas of your life, and observe how balance leads to sustained success and joy.

balance

HAVE YOU EVER FELT LIKE A tightrope walker, carefully treading the line between chaos and order? Life often presents us with seemingly opposing forces: work and play, effort and rest, giving and receiving. The key to a fulfilling existence lies not in choosing one over the other, but in finding the delicate balance between them. Like a scale that's perfectly aligned, allow yourself to embrace both sides of life's equation.

When you feel pulled too far in one direction, gently adjust your stance. Remember, balance isn't about perfection—it's about continuous, mindful adjustments. As you navigate your path, let equilibrium be your guide, helping you maintain steadiness amid life's ebbs and flows.

DEAR UNIVERSE, grant me the wisdom to find balance in all aspects of my life, harmonizing opposing forces with grace and ease.

so be it,
so it is.

harmony

CLOSE YOUR EYES AND IMAGINE A symphony orchestra, each instrument playing its unique part, yet blending seamlessly to create a magnificent whole. This is the essence of harmony in life. Just as every note contributes to the beauty of the music, every experience—both joyful and challenging—adds depth and richness to your journey.

Embrace the discordant moments, for they make the harmonious ones all the sweeter. Seek to align your thoughts, actions, and intentions, creating a melody that resonates with your true self. As you move through your days, listen for the underlying rhythm of life, and allow yourself to flow with it.

DEAR UNIVERSE, help me attune to life's beautiful symphony, finding harmony within myself and with the world around me.

so be it, so it is.

3

align

LIKE A MISALIGNED SPINE CAUSING DISCOMFORT throughout the body, when our actions are out of alignment with our values, we experience tension and unease. Take a moment to reflect: Are your daily choices in harmony with your deepest beliefs and aspirations? Alignment is not about perfection, but about conscious effort to bring your outer world into sync with your inner truth. It's the gentle adjustment of your sails to catch the wind of your purpose.

As you align yourself with your authentic path, you'll find that life begins to flow more effortlessly, obstacles become opportunities, and your energy aligns with the universal current of growth and fulfillment. True manifestation is all about energetic alignment. When I stepped into true alignment with my mission and message of my work, new and exciting opportunities were more magnetically drawn to me.

DEAR UNIVERSE, guide me to align my actions with my highest truth, creating a life of authenticity and purpose.

so be it, so it is.

equilibrium

PICTURE A PENDULUM SWINGING BACK AND FORTH, its arc gradually diminishing until it finds its center point. This natural tendency toward equilibrium is mirrored in our lives. After periods of intense activity or emotion, we instinctively seek balance. Embrace this ebb and flow, recognizing that times of rest are as crucial as times of action. When life tilts you off-center, trust in your innate ability to find your way back.

Cultivate practices that ground you—be it meditation, time in nature, or creative pursuits. These anchors will help you maintain your equilibrium, even when external forces threaten to throw you off balance.

DEAR UNIVERSE, instill in me the strength to maintain my equilibrium amid life's constant changes, finding my center in all situations.

so be it,
so it is.

grace

IN THE DEPTHS OF A TRANQUIL FOREST, a gentle stream flows over smooth stones, its quiet babbling a soothing melody. This is the essence of grace—a state of calm acceptance and inner peace. Grace isn't the absence of storms, but the ability to find stillness within them. It's the quiet strength that allows you to face life's challenges with serenity and equanimity. Cultivate grace by accepting what you cannot change and focusing your energy on what you can influence. Let go of the need to control every outcome, and instead, trust in the natural unfolding of life's journey.

DEAR UNIVERSE, fill my heart with grace, allowing me to navigate life's currents with calm acceptance and inner peace.

so be it,
so it is.

peace

WHAT DOES PEACE MEAN TO YOU? Is it a serene landscape, a quiet moment, or a feeling of contentment deep within? Peace is not just the absence of conflict, but a positive state of being—a harmony between your inner world and outer reality. It's the gentle whisper of your soul when you're living in alignment with your truth. Cultivate peace by releasing what no longer serves you, forgiving yourself and others, and choosing love over fear. As you nurture peace within yourself, watch how it radiates outward, touching every aspect of your life and relationships.

DEAR UNIVERSE, let peace blossom within me, spreading its roots deep and its branches wide, touching all aspects of my life.

so be it, so it is.

7

unity

IMAGINE A TAPESTRY WOVEN FROM COUNTLESS THREADS, each unique in color and texture, yet integral to the overall design. This is the essence of unity—the recognition that we are all interconnected parts of a greater whole. In a world that often emphasizes differences, choose to see the underlying unity that binds us all. Recognize that your actions, no matter how small, ripple out to affect the entire fabric of existence.

Embrace diversity as a strength, understanding that it's our unique contributions that create the rich tapestry of life. As you move through your day, look for opportunities to bridge divides and foster connection.

DEAR UNIVERSE,
open my eyes
to the unity that
underlies all
existence, guiding
me to act with
awareness of our
interconnectedness.

*so be it,
so it is.*

tranquility

HAVE YOU EVER STOOD BY A STILL LAKE AT DAWN, watching the mist rise as the world slowly awakens? This moment of perfect tranquility exists within you always, waiting to be accessed. I remember seeing the water look like glass and feeling this sense of peacefulness wash over all the troubles I was experiencing in my personal life. Tranquility is not something to be found outside yourself, but a state of being you can cultivate from within. It's the calm center that remains untouched by the swirling chaos of daily life. Practice finding this inner stillness through mindfulness, deep breathing, or simply pausing to fully experience the present moment.

As you nurture your inner tranquility, you'll find yourself better equipped to handle life's challenges with grace and poise.

DEAR UNIVERSE, help me cultivate and maintain an inner tranquility that remains steady amid life's ever-changing tides.

so be it,
so it is.

9

symmetry

I'M ONE OF THOSE PEOPLE WHO feels bothered when there is a crooked picture on a wall. I need to create the visual harmony of balance and symmetry but readjusting for symmetry. Nature is an excellent example of how this happens organically.

For instance, in the intricate patterns of a snowflake or the perfect proportions of a seashell, nature reveals its love for symmetry. This balance of form is not just aesthetically pleasing—it's a fundamental principle of the Universe. In your own life, seek to create symmetry between your inner and outer worlds, your aspirations and actions, your giving and receiving. Like a tree that grows both deep roots and high branches, cultivate balance in all aspects of your being.

Remember, true symmetry is not rigid perfection, but a dynamic equilibrium that allows for growth and adaptation based on what you feel and discern is perfect alignment.

DEAR UNIVERSE, guide me to create beautiful symmetry in my life, balancing all aspects of my being in harmony with the natural world.

so be it, so it is.

wholeness

YOU ARE NOT BROKEN, AND YOU do not need fixing. You are a complete and perfect expression of life, exactly as you are in this moment. Wholeness is not a destination to be reached, but a truth to be recognized and lived. Embrace all parts of yourself—the light and the shadow, the strengths and the vulnerabilities. Like a mosaic where each piece, no matter its shape or color, contributes to the beauty of the whole, your perceived flaws and imperfections are integral to your unique magnificence. As you accept and integrate all aspects of yourself, you step into the power of your true wholeness.

Some people seek wholeness through relationships, through their work, and through other external elements of validation. Wholeness is something that will always begin within, and it is something that already exists—you just have to build on it by remembering how incredible you are.

DEAR UNIVERSE, help me embrace my inherent wholeness, integrating all aspects of myself into a beautiful, complete expression of life.

so be it, so it is.

11

coordination

LIFE IS AN INTRICATE DANCE, WITH countless moving parts that must work together in harmony. Like a skilled conductor leading an orchestra, you have the power to coordinate the various elements of your existence into a beautiful symphony. Pay attention to the rhythm of your days, the tempo of your work and rest, the melody of your relationships. When one area of life feels out of sync, gently adjust, always listening for the underlying beat of your authentic self. As you fine-tune your coordination, you'll find a new grace and efficiency in all you do.

DEAR UNIVERSE, grant me the skill to coordinate all aspects of my life into a harmonious whole, moving with grace and purpose.

so be it,
so it is.

fluidity

BE LIKE WATER, MY FRIEND. Water adapts to any container, flows around obstacles, and carves paths through the hardest stone with its gentle persistence. Cultivate this quality of fluidity in your own life. Rigidity leads to brittleness, while flexibility allows for growth and resilience.

When faced with challenges, resist the urge to become rigid or defensive. Instead, soften, adapt, and flow. Trust in your ability to navigate life's twists and turns with grace and ease. Remember, even in stillness, water maintains its essential nature—so too can you remain true to your core while adapting to life's ever-changing currents.

DEAR UNIVERSE, infuse me with the quality of fluidity, allowing me to adapt and flow gracefully through all of life's experiences.

so be it,
so it is.

13

integration

LIKE PUZZLE PIECES COMING TOGETHER TO reveal a beautiful picture, integration is the process of unifying the various aspects of your life into a coherent whole. It's about bridging the gaps between your mind, body, and spirit; between your professional and personal life; between your past, present, and future.

As you work toward integration, you may uncover parts of yourself that have been neglected or hidden. Welcome them with open arms, for true integration requires acceptance of all that you are. As you become more integrated, you'll experience a profound sense of authenticity and alignment in all areas of your life.

DEAR UNIVERSE, guide me toward complete integration, helping me unify all aspects of my being into a harmonious and authentic whole.

so be it,
so it is.

synchronicity

HAVE YOU EVER EXPERIENCED A MOMENT when everything seemed to align perfectly, as if by some cosmic design? These instances of synchronicity are not mere coincidences, but glimpses into the interconnected nature of the Universe. They are invitations to tune in to the subtle rhythms and patterns that surround us. Over the course of my life, I've seen the number 111. I often get people saying they see the clock at precisely 11:11. Instead of the sign needing to have meaning, I tell them to use it as a reminder to pay attention to the magic of the present moment.

As you cultivate awareness of these meaningful coincidences, you'll find yourself flowing more easily with life's current. Trust in the timing of your manifestation journey, knowing that when you are aligned with your true path, the Universe conspires to support you in unexpected and delightful ways.

DEAR UNIVERSE, open my eyes to the synchronicity in my life, guiding me to flow in harmony with the cosmic dance.

so be it, so it is.

calm

IN THE EYE OF A STORM, there is a place of perfect stillness. It's so hard to remember this when you are arguing with your spouse or there's a crisis in your place of business—but calmness is always just a moment of mindfulness away.

This calm center exists within you too, no matter how turbulent your external circumstances may be. It's a reservoir of peace that you can access at any moment, simply by turning your attention inward.

DEAR UNIVERSE, help me cultivate and maintain an unshakeable inner calm, anchoring me amid life's storms and challenges.

so be it, so it is.

Cultivate this inner calm through practices like meditation, deep breathing, or mindful awareness. As you strengthen your connection to this still point within, you'll find yourself better equipped to navigate life's storms with grace and equanimity. Remember, true calm is not the absence of challenges, but the ability to maintain your center amid them.

stability

IMAGINE A MIGHTY OAK TREE, its roots delving deep into the earth, its trunk standing firm against the winds of change. This is the essence of stability—not rigidity, but a grounded flexibility that allows you to bend without breaking. Cultivate your own inner stability by nurturing your core values, building healthy habits, committing to your daily spiritual practice, and maintaining supportive relationships. These become your roots, anchoring you firmly even as you grow and change. With a stable foundation, you can reach higher, take risks, and weather life's storms with confidence, knowing that you have the strength to stand tall through it all.

DEAR UNIVERSE, grant me the strength to build and maintain a stable foundation in my life, supporting my growth and resilience.

so be it,
so it is.

17

vibration

EVERYTHING IS ENERGY. Everything in the Universe is energy in motion, vibrating at different frequencies. Your thoughts, emotions, and actions all emit their own unique vibrations, attracting experiences that match their frequency. Are you conscious of the energy you're putting out into the world? Elevate your vibration by cultivating positive thoughts, expressing gratitude, and aligning your actions with your highest values.

As you raise your frequency, you'll naturally attract more positive experiences and relationships into your life. Remember, you have the power to change your vibration at any moment—choose to resonate with love, joy, and abundance.

DEAR UNIVERSE, help me elevate my vibration, aligning with the highest frequencies of love, joy, and abundance in all aspects of my life.

so be it, so it is.

accord

LIKE MUSICIANS PLAYING IN PERFECT HARMONY, living in accord means aligning your thoughts, words, and actions with your deepest values and aspirations. It's about creating a life where there's no discord between what you believe and how you live. Reflect on the areas of your life where you feel out of tune. Are your daily choices in accord with your long-term goals?

Does your behavior reflect your core values? As you bring the various aspects of your life into accord, you'll experience a profound sense of integrity and authenticity. This inner harmony will radiate outward, creating more harmonious relationships and experiences in your external world.

DEAR UNIVERSE, guide me to live in perfect accord, aligning my thoughts, words, and actions with my highest truth and deepest values.

so be it,
so it is.

19

equanimity

PICTURE A STILL LAKE REFLECTING THE SKY ABOVE, undisturbed by the changing weather. This is equanimity—a state of mental calmness and composure, especially in difficult situations. It's not about suppressing emotions, but about maintaining a balanced perspective that allows you to respond to life's ups and downs with grace and wisdom.

DEAR UNIVERSE, instill in me the quality of equanimity, allowing me to face life's joys and challenges with equal grace and composure.

so be it,
so it is.

Cultivate equanimity by practicing non-attachment to outcomes, accepting what you cannot change, and focusing on what you can control. As you develop this quality, you'll find yourself less swayed by external circumstances and more anchored in your inner peace.

oneness

TAKE A MOMENT TO CONSIDER: Where do you end and the rest of the world begin? The boundary between self and other is more fluid than we often realize. We are all interconnected parts of a greater whole, like waves in the vast ocean of existence.

Embracing this sense of oneness doesn't diminish your individuality; rather, it expands your sense of self to include all of life. As you cultivate this awareness, you'll naturally act with more compassion, understanding that what you do to others, you do to yourself.

Let this realization of oneness guide your interactions, fostering a deeper connection with all beings and with the Universe itself.

DEAR UNIVERSE,
open my heart to the profound truth of oneness, guiding me to live in harmony with all beings and the cosmos.

so be it,
so it is.

21

rhythm

LIFE MOVES TO ITS OWN BEAT, a cosmic rhythm that pulses through all of existence. Are you in step with this divine dance? Pay attention to the natural rhythms in your life—the cycle of day and night, the changing seasons, the ebb and flow of your energy. Honor these rhythms by aligning your activities with them. Just as a skilled dancer moves gracefully by feeling the music, you can navigate life more smoothly by tuning in to its inherent rhythm. Trust in the timing of your journey, knowing that everything unfolds in its perfect rhythm.

DEAR UNIVERSE, attune me to life's sacred rhythms, allowing me to dance in harmony with the cosmic beat that moves through all things.

so be it, so it is.

simplicity

IN A WORLD THAT OFTEN GLORIFIES COMPLEXITY, there's profound and beautiful power in simplicity. Like a clear mountain stream or a single perfect flower, simplicity has its own beauty and strength. Streamline your life by focusing on what truly matters to you. Clear away the clutter—both physical and mental—that distracts you from your essence. This is a wonderful way to clear out the old and make way for the new.

DEAR UNIVERSE, guide me toward simplicity in all aspects of my life, clearing away distractions to reveal the beauty of what's essential.

so be it, so it is.

Simplify your goals, your schedule, your possessions. As you embrace simplicity, you'll find a new clarity of purpose and a deeper appreciation for life's simple pleasures. Remember, simplicity is not about deprivation, but about making room for what's truly important.

23

stillness

IN THE MIDST OF LIFE'S CONSTANT MOTION, have you forgotten the power of stillness? Like a deep, quiet pool reflecting the sky above, stillness allows for clarity and insight that can't be found in constant activity. Make time each day to be still—not just physically, but mentally and emotionally as well. In these moments of stillness, you can hear the whispers of your soul, the subtle guidance of the Universe. As you cultivate stillness, you'll find that it becomes a source of strength and renewal, allowing you to move through life with greater purpose and peace.

DEAR UNIVERSE, help me embrace the power of stillness, finding renewal and clarity in moments of quiet amid life's constant motion.

so be it,
so it is.

serendipity

LIFE IS FULL OF BEAUTIFUL SURPRISES, unexpected connections, and fortunate coincidences. Are you open to receiving these gifts of serendipity? If you are, this is how your manifestations will flow to you throughout life. Cultivate a sense of wonder and curiosity about the world around you. Stay open to possibilities, even when they appear in unexpected packages. Serendipity often occurs at the intersection of preparation and opportunity, so pursue your passions and stay alert to the synchronicities that arise.

Remember, some of life's most precious moments and profound insights come not from careful planning, but from embracing the unexpected. Trust in the magic of serendipity, and watch as life unfolds in delightful and surprising ways.

DEAR UNIVERSE, open my eyes to the serendipitous moments in life, guiding me to embrace the unexpected with joy and wonder.

so be it,
so it is.

25

bliss

CLOSE YOUR EYES AND RECALL A MOMENT OF PURE, unadulterated joy—a moment when you felt completely alive, present, and in harmony with the Universe. This is bliss—a state of perfect happiness and contentment. For me it's been holding my babies in my arms, or when I stand on a beach at dusk and feel the salt air on my face as the full moon rises. Bliss can be anything you want it to be.

While we can't live in constant ecstasy, we can cultivate a deeper sense of joy and fulfillment in our daily lives. Seek out activities that bring you into a state of flow, where time seems to disappear and you're fully immersed in the present moment. Practice gratitude for the simple pleasures of life. As you align more closely with your authentic self and purpose, you'll find that moments of bliss become more frequent, coloring your entire existence with a sense of joy and wonder.

DEAR UNIVERSE, guide me toward experiences of pure bliss, filling my days with joy, wonder, and deep fulfillment.

so be it,
so it is.

elegance

ELEGANCE IS NOT ABOUT EXTERNAL APPEARANCES, but about the grace and simplicity with which you move through life. It's the economy of effort that comes from aligning with your true nature and purpose. Like a skilled dancer who makes complex movements look effortless, cultivate elegance in your thoughts, words, and actions. Strip away the unnecessary, focusing on what's essential. Respond to challenges with poise and dignity.

As you embrace elegance, you'll find that life becomes smoother, more graceful, and more beautiful. Remember, true elegance comes from within—it's a reflection of your inner harmony and authenticity.

DEAR UNIVERSE, infuse my being with elegance, allowing me to move through life with grace, simplicity, and authentic beauty.

so be it, so it is.

27

counterpoise

PICTURE A BABY'S MOBILE HANGING over a crib in perfect balance, each element counterweighting the others to create a harmonious whole. This is counterpoise—a state of equilibrium achieved through the interplay of opposing forces. In your life, seek to create this dynamic balance. Recognize that every aspect of your existence has its counterpart: work and rest, action and reflection, giving and receiving. Instead of seeing these as conflicts, view them as complementary forces that, when balanced, create stability and harmony.

Embrace the full spectrum of your experiences, understanding that joy is deepened by sorrow, strength is forged through challenge, and wisdom comes from both success and failure.

DEAR UNIVERSE, help me achieve perfect counterpoise in my life, balancing all aspects of my being to create harmony and stability.

so be it,
so it is.

frequency

EVERY THOUGHT, EMOTION, and action emits a unique frequency that ripples out into the Universe. What frequency are you tuned in to? Are you broadcasting on a wavelength of fear and scarcity, or love and abundance? Recognize that you have the power to change your frequency at any moment. Elevate your vibration through positive thoughts, acts of kindness, and alignment with your highest values. As you raise your frequency, you'll naturally attract experiences and relationships that resonate with this higher vibration.

Remember, the Universe responds not just to your actions, but to the energy behind them. Tune yourself to the frequency of your deepest aspirations and watch as your reality shifts to match.

DEAR UNIVERSE, attune me to the highest frequencies of love, abundance, and joy, aligning my entire being with my truest aspirations.

so be it, so it is.

synergy

HAVE YOU EVER WITNESSED THE AWE-INSPIRING flight of a flock of birds, moving as one in perfect coordination? This is synergy in action—the creation of a whole that is greater than the sum of its parts. In your own life, look for opportunities to create synergy. Collaborate with others whose strengths complement your own. Align your thoughts, emotions, and actions toward a common purpose. As you cultivate synergy within yourself and in your relationships, you'll discover new levels of creativity, efficiency, and fulfillment.

Remember, true synergy isn't about losing yourself in the collective, but about amplifying your unique gifts through harmonious interaction with others.

DEAR UNIVERSE, guide me to create powerful synergies in all areas of my life, amplifying my potential through harmonious collaboration.

so be it,
so it is.

serenity

SERENITY IS POWERFUL—that state of calm acceptance and inner peace that allows us to navigate life's storms with grace. Serenity is not a destination, but a practice—a continuous choice to release what we cannot control and focus on what we can influence. It's found in the space between acceptance of what is and positive action toward what could be. Cultivate serenity by nurturing your inner calm, practicing mindfulness, and trusting in the unfolding of your journey. As you embrace serenity, you'll find that it becomes a wellspring of strength, allowing you to face life's challenges with equanimity and wisdom.

DEAR UNIVERSE, fill my heart with enduring serenity, granting me the wisdom to accept what I cannot change and the courage to change what I can.

so be it, so it is.

MONTH 12

compassion and kindness

Ending the incredible journey with compassion and kindness reinforces the importance of empathy. This month, we focus on building a supportive and caring community.

Practicing compassion and kindness promotes a sense of connection and well-being, vital for sustained happiness. By fostering empathy, you contribute to a more positive and supportive environment.

REMEMBER: Kindness enriches lives. Practice compassion, spread kindness, and see how your empathy creates an oh-so-beautiful ripple effect of positivity and support.

kindness

HAVE YOU EVER NOTICED HOW A single act of kindness can radiate outward, touching lives far beyond its origin? Kindness is the language that transcends barriers, speaking directly to the heart. It's the gentle hand that lifts another, the warm smile that brightens a stranger's day, the soft word that soothes a troubled soul. As you move through your day, look for opportunities to sprinkle kindness like stardust. Let it be your signature, your legacy. Remember, the kindness you show others not only brightens their world but also illuminates your own path. In a world that can sometimes feel cold, be the warmth that others seek. Your acts of kindness, no matter how small, have the power to change the world, one heart at a time.

DEAR UNIVERSE, guide me to spread kindness like sunlight, touching hearts and illuminating the world with compassion and love.

so be it, so it is.

compassion

IMAGINE YOUR HEART AS A VAST ocean, deep and boundless. Compassion is the tide that rises within you, connecting you to the joys and sorrows of all beings. It's the ability to stand in another's shoes, to feel their pain and share their burdens. Manifest compassion by opening your heart to the world around you. Listen deeply, not just with your ears, but with your entire being. Allow yourself to be moved by the struggles of others, and let that empathy inspire you to act. Remember, compassion is not weakness; it's the ultimate strength that bridges divides and heals wounds. As you nurture compassion within yourself, you become a beacon of hope and healing in a world that desperately needs it.

DEAR UNIVERSE,
fill my heart
with boundless
compassion,
allowing me to
connect deeply
with all beings and
inspire healing.

*so be it,
so it is.*

empathy

CLOSE YOUR EYES AND IMAGINE STEPPING into someone else's life for a moment. What do you see through their eyes? What do you feel in their heart? This is the essence of empathy—the ability to understand and share the feelings of another. It's the bridge that connects us across the chasms of difference, allowing us to see the humanity in everyone we encounter. Activate the power of empathy by listening without judgment, by seeking to understand before being understood.

Let it be the lens through which you view the world, coloring your interactions with understanding and compassion. As you develop this skill, you'll find your relationships deepening, your perspective broadening, and your capacity for love expanding.

DEAR UNIVERSE, enhance my ability to activate the energy of empathy, allowing me to see the world through others' eyes and connect heart-to-heart.

so be it, so it is.

4

generosity

WHAT IF YOU VIEWED EVERYTHING YOU POSSESS—your time, talents, resources—as gifts meant to be shared? Generosity is the art of giving freely, without expectation of return. It's the open hand that offers help, the open heart that shares joy. Like a tree that freely gives its fruit, shade, and beauty, let your life be a continuous offering to the world. Remember, true generosity isn't about the magnitude of the gift, but the spirit in which it's given. Even a kind word or a moment of attention can be a profound act of generosity. As you cultivate this spirit of giving, you'll discover an abundance you never knew you had, for generosity has a way of multiplying what we offer.

DEAR UNIVERSE, fill my heart with boundless generosity, inspiring me to share freely and joyfully all that I have.

so be it,
so it is.

caring

IMAGINE YOUR HEART AS A GARDEN, and caring as the nurturing rain that helps everything grow. Caring is the gentle attention you give to the world around you, the loving consideration that colors your interactions. It's the soft touch that comforts, the attentive ear that listens, the thoughtful gesture that brightens someone's day. Embody the spirit of caring by being present in each moment, attuned to the needs of those around you. Let it infuse your words, your actions, your very being. As you water the garden of your heart with care, watch how it blooms, spreading beauty and fragrance to all who cross your path.

DEAR UNIVERSE, infuse my being to be as caring as possible, allowing me to nurture growth and spread love in all my interactions.

so be it, so it is.

6

benevolence

PICTURE YOURSELF AS A LIGHTHOUSE, standing tall amid the tumultuous sea of life. Your benevolence is the warm, steady light that guides others to safety, offering hope in times of darkness. It's the desire to do good, to bring light where there is shadow, to uplift where there is despair. Manifest the energy of benevolence by choosing kindness in every interaction, by seeking opportunities to make a positive difference, no matter how small. Let your actions be guided by a genuine wish for the well-being of all. As you embrace this spirit of goodwill, you become a beacon of positivity, inspiring others to join you in illuminating the world.

DEAR UNIVERSE, ignite the flame of benevolence within me, guiding me to spread light and goodwill in every corner of life.

so be it, so it is.

sympathy

HAVE YOU EVER FELT THE INVISIBLE thread that connects your heart to another's in times of joy or sorrow? This is sympathy—the ability to share in the emotions of others, to resonate with their experiences. When someone is crying at the airport, for instance, you know they are usually saying goodbye to someone they love. For me that always tugs on the heartstrings.

Like a tuning fork that vibrates in harmony with a nearby sound, let your heart be attuned to the feelings of those around you. Practice sympathy by opening yourself to the emotional landscape of others, by allowing yourself to be touched by their joys and sorrows. Remember, sympathy is not about fixing or changing someone's experience, but about being fully present with them in it. As you develop this quality, you'll find your connections deepening and your understanding of the human experience expanding.

DEAR UNIVERSE,
attune my heart to resonate with others' emotions in genuine sympathy, allowing me to share deeply in life's joys and sorrows.

so be it,
so it is.

8

altruism

IMAGINE A WORLD WHERE EVERY ACTION is motivated by the desire to benefit others. This is the spirit of altruism—the selfless concern for the well-being of others. It's the hand that reaches out to help without thought of reward, the heart that gives freely without expectation of return. Build upon the intention of altruism by looking for opportunities to serve, to make a positive difference in the lives of others. Let it be the driving force behind your choices and actions. Remember, even the smallest act of kindness can have a ripple effect, touching lives far beyond your immediate circle. As you embrace this spirit of selflessness, you'll discover a profound sense of purpose and fulfillment.

DEAR UNIVERSE, inspire me to act with pure altruism, finding joy and purpose in selflessly serving and uplifting others.

so be it, so it is.

humanity

TAKE A MOMENT TO CONSIDER THE vast tapestry of human experience—the joys, sorrows, triumphs, and struggles that unite us all. Humanity is the recognition of our shared journey, the understanding that beneath our differences, we are all part of the same human family. It's the compassion that moves us to help a stranger, the empathy that allows us to celebrate diversity. Activate your sense of humanity by looking beyond surface differences to see the common threads that bind us all. Let it guide your interactions, inspiring you to treat every person with dignity and respect.

As you embrace your shared humanity, you become a bridge-builder, fostering understanding and unity in a diverse world.

DEAR UNIVERSE, deepen my connection to our shared humanity, inspiring me to foster unity and understanding among all people.

so be it, so it is.

10

tenderness

PICTURE A GENTLE STREAM CARESSING the rocks in its path, smoothing their rough edges over time. This is the power of tenderness—the soft, loving care that has the strength to transform. It's the gentle word that soothes a wounded heart, the soft touch that comforts in times of distress.

Build on the energy of tenderness by approaching the world with a soft heart and gentle hands. Let it infuse your words, your actions, your very presence. Remember, in a world that can often feel harsh and unyielding, your tenderness can be a healing balm. As you embrace this quality, you become a sanctuary of gentleness, offering comfort and solace to those around you.

DEAR UNIVERSE, fill my heart with tenderness, allowing me to touch the world gently and bring comfort to those in need.

so be it,
so it is.

warmth

IMAGINE YOURSELF AS THE SUN, radiating warmth and light to all around you. Your warmth is the inviting energy that draws others in, making them feel safe, valued, and cherished. It's the genuine smile that brightens a room, the welcoming embrace that says, "You belong here." Manifest warmth by opening your heart to others, by creating an atmosphere of acceptance and love wherever you go. Let it color your interactions, infusing them with genuine care and affection. As you embody this quality, you become a source of comfort and joy, melting the ice of indifference and lighting up the lives of those you encounter.

DEAR UNIVERSE, let my presence radiate warmth and love, creating a sanctuary of comfort and acceptance for all I encounter.

so be it, so it is.

goodwill

PICTURE YOURSELF AS A GARDENER, scattering seeds of goodwill wherever you go. These seeds are your positive intentions, your kind thoughts, your sincere wishes for the well-being of others. Goodwill is the fertile soil in which understanding grows and conflicts dissolve. It's the open mind that seeks common ground, the generous spirit that assumes the best in others. Cultivate goodwill by approaching each interaction with a genuine desire for positive outcomes for all involved. Let it be the foundation of your relationships and the guiding principle in your dealings with the world. As you sow these seeds of goodwill, watch how they grow into a bountiful harvest of harmony and mutual respect.

DEAR UNIVERSE, fill my heart with abundant goodwill, inspiring me to sow seeds of positivity and understanding in every interaction.

so be it,
so it is.

consideration

HAVE YOU EVER TAKEN A MOMENT to think about how your words and actions affect those around you? True consideration is about thoughtful awareness—the ability to step beyond your own viewpoint and acknowledge the feelings and needs of others. It's in the small gestures: holding the door open, choosing words with care, and going out of your way to make someone feel valued. Cultivate the energy of consideration by practicing mindfulness in your interactions, taking a moment to pause before you speak or act. Let it be the lens through which you filter your intentions, ensuring your impact reflects your good intentions. Embracing this quality creates a ripple of kindness and respect that enriches all your relationships.

When I moved into my new apartment in Green Bay, Wisconsin, in September 2024, I was so absorbed in settling in that I overlooked how my actions might impact my neighbors. My elderly neighbor, who uses a walker, kindly—but firmly—pointed out that my Amazon packages were cluttering the front walkway, making it difficult for her to pass. At first, I felt defensive, but as I thought about her words, I realized they were a reminder to be more considerate. I began paying attention to where I placed deliveries and even offered to help her with her packages when I saw her. This experience taught me that small, thoughtful actions can make a meaningful difference in someone else's day.

DEAR UNIVERSE, heighten my awareness of others' needs, guiding me to act with genuine consideration and thoughtful kindness.

so be it,
so it is.

14

charity

IMAGINE YOUR HEART AS AN OVERFLOWING FOUNTAIN, its waters meant to nourish and refresh those around you. This is the essence of charity—the voluntary giving of help to those in need. It's more than just material assistance; it's the giving of your time, your attention, your compassion. Charity is the hand that reaches out to lift another, the heart that opens to share its abundance. Open your heart to the spirit of charity by looking for opportunities to give, not just from your excess, but from your essence. Let it be an expression of your gratitude for all that you have received. As you embrace this spirit of giving, you'll discover that the more you give, the more your own cup fills, creating a beautiful cycle of abundance and generosity.

DEAR UNIVERSE, open my heart to the joy of giving, inspiring me to share generously and uplift others through acts of charity.

so be it, so it is.

understanding

PICTURE YOUR MIND AS A VAST, clear sky, capable of embracing the full spectrum of human experience. Understanding is the sunlight that illuminates this sky, dispelling the clouds of judgment and ignorance. It's the patient listening that seeks to comprehend before responding, the open mind that welcomes diverse perspectives.

Practice understanding by approaching each situation with curiosity rather than assumption, by seeking to learn rather than to prove yourself right. Let it be the bridge that connects you to others, spanning the gaps of difference and misunderstanding. As you develop this quality, you become a peacemaker, fostering harmony and mutual respect in all your relationships.

DEAR UNIVERSE, expand my capacity for understanding, allowing me to embrace diverse perspectives and foster harmony in all interactions.

so be it, so it is.

16

forgiveness

IMAGINE FORGIVENESS AS A KEY THAT unlocks the chains of resentment and hurt, setting both the forgiver and the forgiven free. Having experienced betrayal firsthand in friendships and relationships, I understand the profound strength it takes to forgive. Forgiveness, for me, has become the gentle rain that washes away the dust of past grievances, allowing new growth to emerge. It's not about condoning harmful actions, but about releasing myself from the burden of carrying anger and pain caused by others. It's the choice to embrace peace over resentment, understanding over judgment. I strive to nurture the energy of forgiveness by acknowledging my own imperfections and extending that same grace to others. It's a gift I give myself, freeing my heart to love more fully, unburdened by the shadows of the past. As I embrace the power of forgiveness, I find a lightness of being—a freedom that allows me to step forward into new possibilities.

DEAR UNIVERSE, grant me the strength of forgiveness, releasing the burdens of the past and opening my heart to new possibilities.

so be it, so it is.

mercy

IN THE GRAND TAPESTRY OF LIFE, mercy is the golden thread that softens the harsh edges of justice with compassion. It's the gentle hand that stays judgment, the kind heart that chooses understanding over retribution. Mercy is not weakness, but a profound strength that recognizes our shared humanity and fallibility. It's the wisdom to know that we all stumble and the grace to help others rise. Manifest the flow of mercy by looking beyond surface actions to see the struggling human beneath. Let it temper your reactions, guiding you to respond with compassion even in challenging situations. As you embrace this quality, you become a source of healing and hope, creating a more forgiving and harmonious world.

DEAR UNIVERSE, fill my heart with boundless mercy, guiding me to respond with compassion and understanding in all situations.

so be it, so it is.

18

grace

PICTURE GRACE AS A GENTLE BREEZE that carries you through life's challenges with poise and dignity. It's the inner strength that allows you to face difficulties with calm assurance, to treat others with kindness regardless of circumstances. Grace is the ability to move through the world with elegance of spirit, to handle both triumph and adversity with equal humility. Embrace grace by nurturing inner peace, by choosing to respond rather than react to life's ups and downs. Let it be the quiet power that infuses your words and actions with beauty and kindness. As you embody grace, you become a calming presence, inspiring others to find their own inner strength and dignity.

DEAR UNIVERSE, infuse my being with grace, allowing me to move through life with poise, kindness, and inner strength.

so be it,
so it is.

patience

HAVE YOU EVER WATCHED A FLOWER slowly unfurl its petals, revealing its beauty in its own perfect time? This is the essence of patience—the ability to wait calmly and trust the natural unfolding of life's processes. Patience is not passive waiting but an active acceptance of the present moment, the quiet understanding that all things bloom in their own season. It's the deep breath you take before responding, the perseverance that keeps you moving forward when results seem distant. Cultivate patience by embracing the journey, savoring each step without fixating on the destination. Let it be the steady rhythm that carries you through both challenges and victories, bringing a new depth of peace and resilience. As you nurture this quality, you'll discover a quiet strength that allows you to stand calmly amid life's storms, confident in the timing of all things.

DEAR UNIVERSE, strengthen in me the virtue of patience, allowing me to trust life's timing and find peace in every moment.

so be it, so it is.

20

heartfelt

IMAGINE YOUR HEART AS A WELLSPRING of genuine emotion, bubbling up and infusing every aspect of your life with authenticity and warmth. To be heartfelt is to live from this deep place of sincerity, to let your true feelings color your words and actions. It's the genuine smile that reaches your eyes, the tears shed in empathy for another's pain, the laughter that comes straight from your soul. Practice a heartfelt approach to life by peeling away layers of pretense and allowing your true self to shine through. Let your interactions be guided by the wisdom of your heart, speaking and acting from a place of genuine care and authenticity. As you embrace this quality, you create connections of profound depth and meaning, touching others with the power of your sincerity.

DEAR UNIVERSE, guide me to live and express myself wholeheartedly, infusing all my interactions with genuine warmth and authenticity.

so be it,
so it is.

gentleness

PICTURE A SOFT FEATHER FLOATING ON a breeze or a dewdrop resting delicately on a leaf. This is the essence of gentleness—the ability to touch the world lightly, with care and sensitivity. Gentleness is not weakness but a refined strength that chooses kindness over force, understanding over judgment. It's the gentle word that soothes a troubled heart that offers comfort and care.

With small children, gentleness becomes even more essential. Their hearts and minds are tender, absorbing every tone, every word, every touch. To be gentle with them is to nurture their spirit and show them that the world is a safe place. But this same gentleness is also needed for ourselves. When we extend the energy of gentleness inward, we allow space for healing, growth, and self-acceptance. Embrace the energy of gentleness by approaching life with a soft heart and a light touch, letting it shape how you treat others and yourself. As you embody this quality, you become a healing presence, creating a safe space for others and yourself to be vulnerable and authentic.

DEAR UNIVERSE, imbue my spirit with gentleness, allowing me to touch the world— and myself—with care and sensitivity, bringing comfort to all I encounter.

so be it,
so it is.

DAY

22

affection

IMAGINE YOUR HEART AS A WARM hearth, radiating affection that draws others close and makes them feel cherished. My seven-year-old daughter, Ava, sometimes gives me random kisses on the cheek, and it's so sweet and unexpected most of the time.

Affection is the language of the heart, spoken through kind words, tender gestures, and loving attention. It's the hug that says, "I'm here for you," the gentle touch that conveys care without words, the warm smile that makes someone feel special. Grow your levels of affection by opening your heart, allowing yourself to express love freely and genuinely. Let it color your relationships, creating bonds of warmth and intimacy.

Remember, in a world that can often feel cold and impersonal, your affection can be a healing balm, nurturing the souls of those around you.

DEAR UNIVERSE,
open my heart to express affection freely, allowing me to nurture others with genuine warmth and loving care.

so be it,
so it is.

nurturing

HAVE YOU EVER WATCHED A GARDENER tenderly care for their plants, giving them water, sunlight, and attention to help them thrive? This is the essence of nurturing—the act of caring for and encouraging growth. Nurturing is the patient hand that guides, the encouraging voice that uplifts, and the steady presence that supports, even in challenging moments. It's about creating an environment where growth feels possible, for both others and ourselves.

To nurture means to listen, to see what someone truly needs, and to offer support tailored to their journey. With children, it's guiding them through emotions and mistakes, or simply spending quality time. And for yourself, it means honoring your own needs with the same care and attention. Allow nurturing to be the foundation of your interactions, fostering resilience and potential in everyone you encounter, including yourself. As you embrace this quality, you become a catalyst for positive change, helping others—and yourself—bloom.

DEAR UNIVERSE, infuse my being with a nurturing spirit, guiding me to support and encourage the growth of all I encounter, including myself.

so be it, so it is.

24

harmony

IMAGINE A RIVER FLOWING GENTLY OVER STONES, winding through forests and fields, adapting to every twist and turn in its path. This is harmony—the state of being in agreement or concord. In life, harmony is about finding balance and alignment, both within yourself and in your relationships with others and the world. It's the ability to blend different elements into a pleasing whole, to find common ground amid diversity. Manifest the energy of harmony by seeking balance in your own life, by being a peacemaker in your relationships, by finding ways to align your actions with your values. Let harmony be the guiding principle that helps you navigate the complexities of life. As you embody this quality, you become a source of peace and unity, creating beautiful music in the symphony of life.

DEAR UNIVERSE, attune me to the rhythms of harmony, guiding me to create balance and unity within myself and in the world.

so be it,
so it is.

support

IMAGINE YOURSELF AS A STRONG, sturdy bridge, providing safe passage for others over troubled waters. This is the essence of support—the act of holding up, bearing the weight, and providing assistance. Support is the encouraging word that bolsters confidence, the helping hand that eases burdens, the steady presence that says, "You're not alone." Improve a supportive nature by being attentive to the needs of others, offering help without judgment or expectation. Let support be a pillar of your relationships, creating a network of mutual care and assistance. Remember, in supporting others, you often find your own strength reinforced. As you embrace this quality, you become a source of stability and comfort, a safe harbor in the storms of life.

DEAR UNIVERSE, strengthen my ability to support others, guiding me to be a steady presence that uplifts and empowers those around me.

so be it, so it is.

26

serenity

CLOSE YOUR EYES AND PICTURE A still lake at dawn, its surface a perfect mirror reflecting the sky above. This is serenity—a state of calm, peaceful tranquility. In life, serenity is the inner stillness that remains unshaken by external turbulence. It's the deep breath that centers you in chaos, the quiet confidence that trusts in life's unfolding. Embody the essence of serenity by practicing mindfulness, by learning to respond rather than react to life's challenges. Let serenity be the calm core at the center of your being, a wellspring of peace you can always return to. As you embody this quality, you become a calming presence in the world, offering others a glimpse of the peace that resides within us all.

DEAR UNIVERSE, fill my being with deep serenity, allowing me to remain calm and centered amid life's storms.

*so be it,
so it is.*

empathetic

IMAGINE YOUR HEART AS A FINELY tuned instrument, capable of resonating with the emotions of those around you. This is empathy—the ability to understand and share the feelings of another. Empathy is the bridge that connects hearts across the chasms of difference, allowing us to truly see and understand one another. It's the listening ear that hears not just words but the feelings behind them, the compassionate heart that feels another's joy or pain as its own. Lean into empathy by practicing active listening, by putting yourself in others' shoes, by allowing yourself to be touched by the experiences of those around you. Let empathy guide your interactions, fostering deeper connections and understanding. As you embrace this quality, you become a healing presence in the world, creating spaces of genuine connection and mutual understanding.

DEAR UNIVERSE, deepen my capacity for being empathetic, allowing me to truly understand and connect with the hearts of others.

so be it, so it is.

28

giving

PICTURE YOURSELF AS AN ABUNDANT FRUIT TREE, branches heavy with ripe fruit meant to be shared. This is the spirit of giving—the act of freely transferring the ownership of something to someone else. Giving is more than just material gifts; it's the offering of your time, your attention, your love, your unique gifts and talents. It's the smile freely given to a stranger, the listening ear offered to a friend in need, the helping hand extended without expectation of return. Invite a giving spirit by recognizing the abundance in your own life and finding ways to share it with others. Let giving be a natural expression of your gratitude and love. As you embrace this quality, you'll discover that the more you give, the more you receive, creating a beautiful cycle of abundance and joy.

DEAR UNIVERSE, open my heart to the joy of giving, guiding me to share freely and abundantly from all that I have and all that I am.

so be it, so it is.

tenderhearted

IN 1987, WHEN I WAS SEVEN YEARS OLD, Care Bears were all the rage. My cherished Care Bear was Tenderheart, adorned with a heart on his belly. The heart has always been a powerful symbol throughout society. In fact, during the writing of my memoir *Be the Love* in 2020, I tattooed a tiny heart on my right wrist as a personal emblem of self-love.

Imagine your heart as a soft, warm blanket, ready to envelop others in comfort and care. To be tenderhearted is to approach the world with a gentle, loving sensitivity. It's the capacity to be deeply moved by others' joys and sorrows, responding with genuine care and compassion. A tenderhearted person acts as a healing balm in a world that often feels harsh and uncaring.

To nurture tenderheartedness, allow yourself to feel deeply and respond to others with authentic warmth and care. Let your heart remain soft and receptive while maintaining your inner strength. As you embrace this quality, you become a wellspring of comfort and healing, touching lives with your sincere care and sensitivity.

DEAR UNIVERSE, soften my heart to be tenderhearted, allowing me to respond to the world with genuine warmth, care, and sensitivity.

so be it,
so it is.

30

heartfulness

ENVISION YOUR HEART AS A BOUNDLESS reservoir of warmth and light, embracing all of life's experiences with sincerity and love. This is heartfulness—living with an open, intentional heart, fostering genuine care and connection.

Heartfulness combines mindfulness with compassion, bringing love into action. It's the gentle touch, kind words, and steady presence that uplifts and soothes.

Cultivate heartfulness by practicing gratitude, offering kindness, and seeing the shared essence of all beings. Let your heart inspire acts of care and generosity, spreading ripples of healing and harmony into the world.

DEAR UNIVERSE, expand my soul with boundless heartfulness, inspiring me to understand deeply and act kindly to alleviate suffering wherever I encounter it.

so be it,
so it is.

love

WHAT IF YOU VIEWED LOVE NOT just as an emotion, but as a state of being? Love is the highest form of consciousness. Love, in its purest form, is the essence of who you are. It's the force that connects all beings, the energy that creates and sustains life. Love is not just romantic affection, but the unconditional acceptance and care for all of existence. It's the smile that brightens a stranger's day, the forgiveness that heals old wounds, the kindness that expects nothing in return.

Manifest love by opening your heart wide, by choosing to see the beauty and worth in all beings. Let love be the lens through which you view the world, coloring all your thoughts, words, and actions. As you embody this quality, you become a beacon of light in the world, spreading the transformative power of love to all you encounter.

DEAR UNIVERSE, let love flow through me abundantly, guiding my every thought, word, and action to spread light and healing in the world.

so be it,
so it is.

ACKNOWLEDGMENTS

and gratitude

Writing this book has been a profound journey, and I'm filled with so much gratitude for the many wonderful people who have supported and inspired me along the way.

To my agent, Jaidree Braddix, and the exceptional team at Park & Fine Literary and Media: Thank you for believing in my vision and guiding me through the intricacies of bringing this book into the world. Your expertise and dedication have been invaluable.

Emma Effinger, my incredible editor, and everyone at Harvest / HarperCollins: Your hard work and care in shaping this book have been truly appreciated. Emma, your insightful suggestions and meticulous attention to detail have elevated this work in ways I couldn't have imagined.

To my parents, Tony Prout and Louise Findlay: Your unwavering love, support, humor, and strength have been the foundation of everything I've accomplished. I'm deeply grateful to have you both in my life.

Jon: Your unconditional love, support, wisdom, and presence in my life mean more than words can express. You're my star.

To my beloved children, Thomas, Olivia, Lulu, and Ava: You are my world. Your love and light inspire everything I do, and I am so proud to be your mother. This book, like all things, is for you.

My dear friend Catherine Murphy: Thank you for always being there, supporting me through every chapter—both in life and in writing. Your kindness and friendship are a true blessing.

And to my readers, *Manifest* podcast listeners, mentoring clients, and manifestation students: Your support means everything to me. Thank you for being a part of this journey. I hope this book brings as much inspiration to you as you've brought to me.

INDEX

DEAR UNIVERSE 365. Copyright © 2025 by Sarah Prout. All rights reserved.
Printed in India. No part of this book may be used or reproduced in any manner whatsoever
without written permission except in the case of brief quotations embodied in critical articles
and reviews. For information, address HarperCollins Publishers, 195 Broadway, New York,
NY 10007. In Europe, HarperCollins Publishers, Macken House, 39/40 Mayor Street Upper,
Dublin 1, D01 C9W8, Ireland.

HarperCollins books may be purchased for educational, business, or
sales promotional use. For information, please email the Special Markets
Department at SPsales@harpercollins.com.
hc.com

FIRST EDITION

DESIGNED BY RENATA DE OLIVEIRA

Illustrations by Katelyn Morse
Illustration on page i by Yasnarada/shutterstock

Library of Congress Cataloging-in-Publication Data
has been applied for.

ISBN 978-0-06-342620-7

MAI